Raising the Global Mindset

Parenting Essays by Thought Leaders
Around the World to Empower Children

Curated by

Aditi Wardhan Singh

For permission requests or bulk discounts, write to the publisher, addressed "Attention: Permissions Coordinator," at the address - contact@raisingworldchildren.com

© **2020 Aditi Wardhan Singh**
Raising World Children LLC

Paperback - ISBN-13: 978-1-7335649-6-0
Hardcover - ISBN-13: 978-1-7335649-7-7

LCCN Number - 2020922026

FREE companion items to this book including antiracism education resources, children's books and related lesson plans are available at RaisingWorldChildren.com

Writers around the world are welcome to submit their articles or inquire about our next collaborative book at contact@raisingworldchildren.com

Contents

THOUGHT LEADERS FEATURED IN THIS BOOK

Sneha	Sindhuja	Jewel	Shannon	Sybil
Purvi	Lup Wai	Sherry	Devishobha	Nupur
Briana	Aditi	Minali	Dilraz	
Sangeetha	Johana	Shalini	Flor	Rivkah
Madhu	Lucretia	Josephine	Maureen	Ronda

INTRODUCTION

REINTRODUCE YOURSELF TO THE WORLD

The world is a melting pot, and yet we are all living in our own little worlds.

Every family is multicultural in some respect, either directly or by association. Our children can benefit from the tapestry that is woven constantly around them with the multiple threads of cultures, languages, people, and more. And yet many families focus solely on their own heritage or subculture of home, neglecting to let their children experience the world in all it's beauty. Either out of fear of losing their identity or because we are just too overwhelmed and do not have the time to engage with the learning that is needed.

The truth is that today humanity is sinking in our worries, in the daily grind, in the day to day needs of those around us, in fears of the unknown. We make up excuses of being busy for every moment we neglect to be mindful in our choices.

This "busyness" also keeps us from coming up for air, to have the time to look up and care. For our friends, current issues and challenges of people different from us.

We have all, time and again been guilty of being too self-involved, spending what little free time we have on social media. Succumbing to confirmation bias, which grows stronger when we keep clicking on all that which constantly supports our world view. We neglect to go looking for resources that challenge our pre-existing beliefs.

That is why many feel strong emotions, when one person sees a 6, where another sees a 9. People get offended or hurt quite easily, not remembering that we are all inherently different.

We forget that while we may all often find ourselves in the same boat, the resources we have at hand, our origin and destination are all different.

Sympathy is easy to drum up in obvious circumstances like loss or failure but empathy, that needs a whole different skill set. To understand another's perspective with that inherent knowledge: that the paths you have come from and are on are entirely different.

The many cultural insensitivities, appropriation, and the inappropriate remarks we notice or let slide and/or are hurt by, are often made from a place of ignorance or denial. Over our lifetime, we have all even made many such remarks or been thoughtless, not realizing we have mirrored the very behavior we do not appreciate in others.

For example, when people speak in their native language, they hope to build a community within their language peers, unwittingly making those around them feel left out.

Though, is it fair to penalize ignorance? I believe not.

After all, our world view, the stereotypes, and habits we subconsciously develop, the attitude that we project; are all honed over years of observation of the behavior of those around us. The content we have consumed and the conversations we have lent ears to, have shaped our subtle behavioral attributes.

How should we then provide our kids with tools to broaden their world view? How do we teach them about something we lack?

It takes conscious effort!

We desire to raise kids, are kind, are strong and mindful in their choices and constantly aware of possible consequences to those around them. But how do we empower our children, when we ourselves are so lost in our personal bubbles?

It takes constant learning and acknowledgement that we will never know enough. That we can grow daily, if only we choose to raise our mindset to the global level.

Why This Book?

Do we even need to raise our mindset to a global level?

To break your bubble. To crack stereotypes. To widen your global circle.

I am always asked, "Where in India are you from?" and "Are you Bengoli?" Most new people I met over my lifetime have asked me either of these two questions. I do not consider myself only from India, and I never knew what a Bengoli stereotypically looked like, till very recently (never having met one).

I knew why they were asking me though. People want to box everyone they meet into a category that they are comfortable with.

If it was a box they had already experienced and were comfortable with, I was welcomed into their world with open arms. Given the benefits reserved for people of their community (Maharashtra, Madhya Pradesh, Kuwait, Mumbai, Gulf or Hindu).

The truth is, it is often people who never asked me either question that became a part of my world. It is those people who know that it did not matter where I was from, only who I was on the inside.

This book and the people inside it help you raise such humans. People who see a person for who they are, and not where they are from or what they look like.

I think it is more important to be the conduit by which someone expands their world view. To be a resource for diversity and help break stereotypes gently, by going out of our own comfort zones.

If you have gotten this far, I thank you for making the conscious effort needed to build up our children and give them a better world.

Anti-racism education does not have to be a " Let's sit down and have a conversation about 'Diversity and Inclusion'" but more a "Let's look at the world and all it holds in a new light" approach. To be a sponge ourselves, so that our kids can soak up what comes their way.

Have you ever thought of the pressure parents have on raising multicultural children to be global citizens?

And when I say multicultural, I mean kids being raised in different cultures owning to expat life, interracial, interreligious, immigrant life, disabilities, and/or any situation that makes them more than they are.

Challenges of a Multicultural Family

- Preserving the mother tongue.

- Learning a new language to build a local community.

- A parent being confused for a caregiver.

- Preserving the culture per heritage or religion.

- Dealing with daily microaggressions.

- Teaching kids to be respectful of other cultures.

- Pressures from extended family to carry on traditions.

- Balancing the old world and new.

- Building an identity for the kids that helps them grow confidence and empathy.

- Developing cultural empathy to know the difference between appropriation and appreciation.

- Being mindful about their own intergenerational biases and consciously unlearning them.

And all this, while creating a world of their own that fits their little family. A world that helps children keep their feet planted in all the borders they are part of.

Diversity and Inclusion are Beautiful Gifts

We are all different and that is beautiful. Our similarities connect us.

Our differences - the culture, the experiences we have had, the upbringing make every single one of us unique.

We are raising our children in a world where even people in the same culture have different perspectives towards the world. To give our children a better understanding of the world they are living in, we need to expand our own mindset towards what we already know.

People often talk about how we are all different on the outside but same on the inside.

One of the things I have been trying to do with my own children is undo this narrative. We are **not** all the same on the inside. Each person has a different set of gifts and a different background that might include things you do not understand (trauma, racial barriers, neurodiversity, etc.).

It is important to teach children that as humans, we all have so much in common, but it is also important to teach them that our life experiences may be significantly different, because of how we are treated based on our skin color. Same and Different.

Do not be colorblind to erase different histories, experiences, opportunities and rights.

Did you know some of the many themes within diversity?

- Cultural
- Racial
- Religious
- Age
- Sex/Gender
- Disability

And this is not counting the subdivisions within each. Raising awareness about all these kinds of divisions and dealing with them means being consciously aware of the four diversity type dimensions - Internal, External, Organizational, and World View.

All these get embedded within a child, as we expose them to a world full of stories by people different than them, within and outside their immediate community. Our job as parents is to teach kids to be kind and respectful, and to lend an ear to other people's stories.

And that is where this book comes into the picture. The thought leaders in this book do a fabulous job of providing you strategies and perspectives, unique to the work they are doing within their unit, organization, or family to build a global mindset.

Raising the Global Mindset - for Our Children

During the pandemic of 2020, we have seen differences open like chasms as never before. Especially on or because of social media. Emotions run high and fingers type with rage, fueled by misinformation. It is our duty as parents to reduce the divide and not let it affect our children.

To protect them. To empower them. Especially, with the isolation they experienced during the past few months, where our bubbles had been reduced to four walls and a screen.

It means taking on the responsibility for what we do not know about the world. To be a student willing to learn from everyone you meet. To willingly look for the opposite point of view and what formed it. To be open to conversation and the healthy debate that ensues. To build a mindset that can look at every situation from many people's perspective.

Also, understanding means consciously diversifying our world by exploring the world in a million ways, and not the monochrome of our own culture.

Each thought leader in this book had done exactly that. Given you a starting point. Every chapter is a world full of encouragement and personal growth, should you choose to look and apply those to your own life.

Be warned. You may find a lot of repetitive advice in this book, because -

a) great minds think alike.

b) repetition needs to be the foundation of conversation around antiracism, diversity, and inclusion.

c) it only goes to show how important those points are.

Together, a **group of powerful women** have come together to give you the gift of being able to look at every situation from the perspective of many people, all at once.

This book and others like it, give you a peek into the lives of multicultural families around the world, and fills that void in your life which allows you to be conscious about broadening your world view.

Let us enrich our families and empower our children to grow into empathetic visionaries who are confident in identity, rooted in heritage and powered by wings of a worldview.

Section I
Understanding
the
Multicultural Family

Chapter 1

Being a Third Culture Kid
Dilraz Kunnummal

"So, here you are
Too foreign for home
Too foreign for here
Never enough for both."
- Ijeoma Umebinyuo

"Where are you from?" is a question I often get. Despite having answered it a million times, I still am conflicted about the response. *"Where am I from?"* Do they mean my nationality or where I was born or where I grew up or where I live now? You know! The simple challenges of being a lifelong expat!

I am Indian by origin, born and raised in a tiny island kingdom called Bahrain, and currently call Qatar home. Am I an Indian? Absolutely, but not quite. Am I a Gulfie? Absolutely, but not quite...I guess I am both. I am a true-blue 'Gulfie Desi', who is married to another Gulfie Desi born and raised in Dubai. And together we are raising the next generation Gulfie Desi in the beautiful land of Doha.

Being an expat is all I have ever known – and it seeps into your identity. India is as much a part of my identity, as is the place where I was born and raised in, and as well as the one where my child is thriving now.

One thing I must say about expats is that somehow being away from the homeland brings you together and binds you in a way that no other relationship can. Even without any pressure, you are inclined to learn more about the various heritage and traditions of the community that surrounds you. And India – with its multitude of ethnicities and languages – means that all Desi gatherings become a true melting pot.

Being an expat and being in proximity with others who have not been raised with the same customs and rituals broadens your horizons. It helps you become a lot more open-minded and teaches inclusivity and respect.

Almost every year for the past decade and beyond, my family and I have celebrated Indian festivals such as Diwali and Navratri. We have dressed up in ornate *lehengas* and *kurta-pyjamas*, enjoyed mouth-watering dishes ranging from *Butter chicken* to *RoganJosh* – all not a part of my South-Indian culture. And I have had many of my non-South Indian friends enjoy donning the kasavu-sari and relish enjoying a scrumptious *Onam Sadya*. Sometimes, I truly feel that I have revelled in my Indianness a lot more than my extended family, who were born and raised in India.

The most effective way to teach a child about culture is to actively participate in it and not force any aspect of it. We must give them opportunities to practice and promote it by practicing it ourselves, without letting it overtake every other element in their life.

I was fortunate to be raised in a house which never saw an enforcement of tradition. There was no pressure to learn the language or eat the food! But Malayalam was spoken at home and I can now speak it fairly well, though my reading skills are self-taught, and my writing is minimal.

Rice and other typical dishes were regular staples at lunch time. I remember growing up not wanting to eat rice and curries at all. But these days, I absolutely must have a classic Kerala meal at least once a week. Neither did I expect that nor did I realize when that disdain turned into a craving!

Another element of my childhood I am truly thankful for is my dance lessons. I have learnt Indian classical dance forms including *Bharatnatyam, Mohiniyattam and Kuchipudi* for over a decade – again something that I was not fully convinced about – but a key part of who I am today. To be honest, learning these dance forms were almost unheard of where my parents grew up, but they wanted to help me go beyond their experiences.

I am told I speak particularly good Hindi – *for a non-native speaker*. Do you want to take a wild guess at who my teacher was? Bollywood movies, believe it or not! We did have Hindi in school, but that was not enough to learn it to converse in it. It was indeed my Wednesday night Bollywood flick that came on the local Bahrain TV that was my guru. Since then, I have had the platforms to polish it because I have lived in Bombay and Pune, but who would have thought Bollywood movies could have such positive influences too?

Growing up, that is what stands out. The exposure to the various elements of a culture that my parents knew of – not even one they fully grew up in. The beauty of being part of the Indian diaspora is that you never really feel like you have left home. We are everywhere! Have you heard the inside joke we Indians make? "Go to the moon, and you'll see a small tea stall run by Indians." Sometimes, I think that may possibly be true. As someone who went to an Indian school, and then went for extra-curricular activities at a *desi* club, I feel grateful.

The exposure alone is not enough. It was also my parents' constant attempts to give us a platform and opportunities to participate in activities related to our culture. It was hearing my mom talk about some amazing Indian writers, and seeing folklore come alive though theater and dance. It was growing up thinking "this seems like a fun thing to try," and not "I must do this or else…"

While it is crucial that you introduce elements of your original culture, it is also as important to allow children to learn from the culture of the place they will essentially call home. Be it the cuisine, clothing or rituals – explore these too with the same respect and value it as yours.

Every year, we would wait for Bahrain's National Day, and deck up in our winter best, and watch the fireworks. We would stand along with expats from around the world including NRIs (Non-Resident Indians), waiting with bated breath to watch the festivities that celebrate the nation's independence.

And now with my child, every year without fail, we have celebrated *Garangao* – a children's festival that comes right in the middle of Ramadan – something that is rarely found outside of the *Middle East*. And he is already learning Arabic at school.

We wore *lehengas* and *salwar khameez*, and *abayas* and *thobes* – just the same. All good news would be accompanied with *laddoos* or *jalebis* or *baklava*! The Old Souq will always be a place that I cherish. We enjoyed a good shawarma as much as we would enjoy *idli* and *chutney*. In fact, that is one of the things we miss when we go to India or elsewhere – a good shawarma!

Fun story about moving to India: When I started university in Pune, I used to love running out in the rains. It was magical! Because growing up in a desert country, all we had were a few drizzles. But even those little bits of rain had us running out in raincoats, boots, and umbrellas. People thought we were crazy.

I always loved going to India when I was a child. And I thoroughly enjoyed the 5+ years I spent at university. But did I belong there? I do not know. But did I belong in the land I often called home? That too is blurred.

So, who am I? That bit is crystal clear.

I am indeed a third culture kid. I am someone, who embraced every bit of my various identities and has made it my own.

The myriad of bits and pieces of my identity - where I am from, and where I call home came together to form a beautiful jigsaw that fits together perfectly, one that is unique and irrevocably mine.

And you too can raise an empowered individual who celebrates their various identities. Someone who can also enable other third-culture kids to find their ground and navigate through the plethora of inspirations – by allowing them to fully explore their roots. And by roots, I do indeed mean both the origin and home country.

Often, we forget that our children are not us and they are not growing up in our world – but in one of their own.

Let them build their own culture, infused with elements of every place they have been to. Let them soar knowing that they are not just from one country but indeed of the world. This is important – for we are not raising Indian Americans, or any single nationality – we are raising *World Children*.

Kids are raised to be confident and empowered *third culture kids* when we -

1. Expose them to various elements of both cultures (origin country and home country) through language, arts, literature, cuisine, and clothing, among others.

2. Actively participate, represent, and celebrate the traditions and cultures of both places.

3. Do not enforce any element of culture on our child. Be involved and model it, and the children will pick it up.

4. Give both cultures, traditions and practices the respect and value it deserves. It may be different, but do not place one over the other.

5. Allow children to build their own culture infused with elements of all the places they call home.

ABOUT DILRAZ KUNNUMMAL

Author of the bestselling children's book See You Soon, Dilraz Kunnummal is a journalist with multicultural influences. Born and raised in the Middle East and mom to a 4-year-old, she is committed to raising a global citizen through conscious parenting. She has dabbled in various media industries including radio, television, online and print across various genres. From anchoring to a crowd of more than 5000 people, to being the first face of a Malayalam TV show telecast from Bahrain, from writing poetry to having a popular mom blog, from choreographing award winning dance performances to being invited on the BBC to share her viewpoints as an expat journalist, she has done it all! An advocate for pursuing dreams even after motherhood, her book **See You Soon** teachers families to deal with the separation anxiety, both toddlers and mothers feel.

Website: https://mommydil.com

Instagram: https://instagram.com/Dilknml

Chapter 2

Multicultural Family Problems
Josephine O'Brien

*"We cannot solve our problems with the same
thinking used when we created them."*
– Albert Einstein

Identity is more about how we as individuals view ourselves as unique from others. As a family, our identity was originally constituted by our race and culture. This identity has been evolving progressively at personal and social levels along with movement and acculturation.

Identity is also perceived as dynamic since it is established and shaped in interaction, which is necessary to understand how communication works in diverse situations.

In any given society, differences between individuals are much greater than differences between groups. **Education, personal opinions, religion, character, experience, emotions, attitudes and numerous other factors all contribute to what can be called 'personal identity'.**

To successfully socialize in our diverse society requires us to draw from our experiences of appropriate behavior and cultural expectations.

Families with different races or nationalities face unique challenges. They are dealing with different languages, customs, religions, beliefs, and lifestyles daily. Various sayings and gestures may mean different things in different cultures. This may lead to different levels of misunderstanding or confusion.

Therefore, couples that do not share a common background, such as, religion, language, education, economic status, nationality, and values may not understand their partner's belief and behavior system.

What makes a family multicultural?

The composition of families is adjusting to the changes in our society, observed particularly in our learning settings. Many students are children of, or are former immigrants themselves. The demographics of our world are often overlooked, to the point that broader diversity discussions are now of crucial importance.

In our case, multicultural family means multiracial, bilingual, bicultural, working towards biliterate in English and Arabic and various other levels of difference. Our immediate family lives on both sides of the globe and neither family speaks the other family's language or shares their religion. We are raising children to identify and assimilate in both my husband's and my culture, regardless of which side of the globe we live. Others define a multicultural family in terms of world schooling and learning about other countries, cultures, religions, and attending festivals or celebrations in the cities where they live - to extend their food and cultural experiences.

A Learning Curve for a Multicultural Family.

A wise owl once told me that to define our issues as problems was just asking for more problems. 'Problems' belong in math class, so kindly leave them there! If you identify problems as opportunities and give them a goal, it is a far more productive enterprise.

At first, I dismissed it as more unsolicited advice, smiled sweetly whilst trying not to roll my eyes as I walked away. As luck would have it, I walked away into a lesson of discovery. I did the unthinkable! This white Australian girl advised her predominantly Christian family and friends that she would be marrying a person from the other side of the world. I was to marry a refugee, whose family does not speak English and are all Muslim. I told my family that he is biliterate, an academic and ESL teacher, does not share their religion or skin color, and we will be raising our children in our shared religion. Following it up with 'it is our intention that our children will be biliterate and bicultural to ensure they grow up secure in their identity'.

Australia is predominantly a Christian country. I grew up in a Christian household but at university met a group of friends that led me to Islam and my husband. My husband grew up in the Middle East in a Muslim household before fleeing his country and arriving in Australia as a refugee. It was a shock to my Australian family, when I firstly married a Muslim man and then said we were raising our children to follow Islam. I maintain we all worship the one God, who in Arabic is called by the Arabic word for God, "Allah". With my husband's family all residing in some part of the desert in the Middle East, if my children wanted to traverse two cultures, then they needed to learn the culture of their part of the desert. Islam is their way of living and it is not just the religion of this part of the Middle East.

Wow! The naysayers quickly drowned out the few who thought this goal was not a dream based solely in my imagination.

I took the pragmatic approach – I am a trained pilot and the biggest thing I learnt from this exercise is that half of your training is not about how to fly the plane but being prepared for emergencies. Trusting in what you know. The emergency checklist in nearly all cases ensures a safe landing. Therefore, it was time for a brainstorming session with my co-pilot (husband). What was going on that emergency checklist?

Things to Consider -

Children's names

The names chosen need to be easily pronounceable and meaningful for both families. Not, inadvertently choosing a name that has bad karma in one language or the other.

Religion

The religion of the country? Or the religion of your family?

We chose the religion of our family, Islam. The motto which explains why our extended family has two religions but are happy together is: "We worship one God, known in English as God and Allah in Arabic."

However, we also choose to have our children participate with my parents and family in Australian festivals and religious feast days. We explain why we don't celebrate these days but they are important to their grandparents so must be respected.

We also make a point of introducing our children to other friends' religions and teach them to be understanding and respectful.

I always try to encourage "knowledge, understanding and respect." We try to live by, *"You don't have to agree, but you do have to be respectful!"*

What language/languages will you use?

Bilingual, biliterate, or a combination of both? Is one language to be more dominant than the other? Alternatively, are you going to invest energy in keeping them equal?

How are you going to teach/learn the languages you choose for your family?

My investigation showed that OPOL (one parent one language) is the most common teaching method for bilingual families, but my husband was working and studying long hours so I have facilitated

11

as much as possible the learning of both languages. Also, he assists as much as possible when time permits him. Being biliterate and bilingual has always been our goal for our children.

How does a non-native speaker help teach a partner's language?

• We used a partly immersion style of learning.

• A particular time devoted to Arabic each day.

• Books and different types of learning/ teaching materials are available.

• Online YouTube cartoons and videos.

• Satellite tv for news and sports.

• Learning to sing songs from DVDs with subtitles on.

• Making a word/picture wall for learning.

• Making playing cards and craft.

• Encourage enthusiasm for learning even when you struggle yourself.

• Encourage New language to be used with video links to the family.

• When their dad's car was pulling in, if our children were awake, I put on Arabic cartoons. Their dad heard Arabic, so it prompted him to speak Arabic with our children, not English.

School time - a new adventure

When your children enter school is when you need a sense of humor the most. Here is why...

First the issue of figuring out which one of the below you are going to admit your child in -

• Public school

• Private school

• Dual language school

• Single language school and a tutor and/or afterschool language lessons

• Montessori, Warldof...

We decided preschool in English as the school was close to home, Immersion in Arabic at home, followed by dual-language school would meet the language needs of our family. We also enrolled in some extra language lessons, when my husband's study and work did not allow sufficient time to put in the extra language hours required.

In Australia, some non-profit organizations run schools for teaching Arabic and Islam. At public school, one lesson a week is taught of a religion or an ethics course if you choose not. In private schools, you have a choice of religion as the school is usually attached to a church or mosque. Our decision was to enroll our children in an Islamic College for school, where the ethics were the principles of Islam, and our children received instruction in Arabic as a second language (so they also learnt to speak Arabic not just read and write it).

Beyond everyone wanting to explain why this was the wrong decision for school, when your family is biracial (I am Australian with Irish/English ancestry, very white, and my husband is Middle Eastern Arab and very dark – our children are very lightly tanned) and bicultural, you end up with the question of *"Is your husband really the children's father?"* Besides the fact, the administrator asking the question has their birth certificate in her hand and it is not legal for her to ask such a question. Sorry, all I can say on that one is get used to it! Deep breath, and sense of humor required!! My usual response is *"Do you ask everyone who walks through the door that question?"* That became the least of my worries!

Issue number two, which still stuns me every time it happens because it was nowhere near an isolated incident. The first day my husband collected my daughter from school – my daughter was over the moon excited her dad would collect her. I made sure to advise the teachers in the morning. 3pm arrives with a panicked call from the teacher.

No hello, nothing...just *"What does your husband look like?"* I was somewhat confused answering her worried tone, implying a catastrophe at school, *"Tall, about 6 feet...he is a pretty big guy, ask our daughter she will show you. What happened?"* Still sounding worried but she says *"Um, it's just that…"* then I hear my daughter's voice, *"Miss, Miss, it's Baba!"* Then it dawns on me. No one has read my daughter's file. Into the phone I say, *"Excuse me, are you there?"* The reply, *"Um, yes?"* I took a deep breath and managed to politely say, *"The 6-foot tall, big, black guy standing in front of you is my husband and 'Baba' is Arabic for Dad. If you had bothered to read my daughter's file, you would find a photo and these details. If you had however asked for his identification to check the file (which is protocol for an unknown visitor), you would know already that the man is my daughter's English and Arabic speaking father. Kindly, show him how to sign her out and send them home."*

On that day, I was so shocked and stunned, I was still crying when my husband arrived home. Try explaining that one to your spouse politely. I think what more horrifying was that he took one look at my tears and said, *"You don't need to say anything. It is ok. I worked out they were stunned and panicking over who I was. That was why I sat down and waited. Then they had the time to talk to you. I figured it was just easier for all."* I don't know how you respond to one's husband's acceptance that it will always happen.

Nearly fifteen years of marriage and nine years of children at school later and I still do not get it!

That was preschool, not a thing changed when my kids went to school. And here I was thinking the most worrying part of school was going to be helping my kids become biliterate.

Our conclusion checklist

The most important lesson we learnt through the midst of these challenges was to always remain true to our family. When circumstances called into question the why and how of our family plan, we always remembered our family goal "that our children will be able to speak to both their grandmothers in their grandmother's language with no translator required".

This was the only point that was of real importance! After discussions with my husband and consideration of all the above factors, we settled on a checklist that works for us and might work for others, with some changes or amendments based on their circumstances.

- Encourage daily learning in both languages
- Read daily in both languages
- Either write or copy a passage each day in both languages
- Ensure all homework for school is completed
- Attend festivals and cultural events in your city - we participate in Christmas and Easter activities with my family whilst explaining to our children why our family does not celebrate these feast days
- Learn to cook food from both cultures
- Speak to grandparents via video chat regularly
- Encourage children to have the confidence to embrace both their cultures
- Never lose sight of your goal - no matter the problems presented

I always carry my goal written in my wallet as a reminder for the times I find unsolicited advice difficult.

Finally, just to remember your goal! Find a piece of paper and write it down. A flexible goal that works for you and your special family. It does not need to be perfect; it just needs to be readable and work for your family!

ABOUT JOSEPHINE O'BRIEN

Josephine is an Australian. Accountant by trade. Teacher by necessity. Advocating for learning differences, gifted, and multiliterate children. She grew up on a farm in country NSW, where she developed a love for languages hosting Japanese farm stay visitors, and as an exchange student. Studied several languages whilst working and met her Arabic speaking husband at University. Currently an expat, world schooling in an effort to provide a holistic approach to bicultural.

Her current projects involve researching second language learning as a tool for assisting dyslexic children with reading and writing and starting to blog in Arabic to encourage her children's writing skills. Crafting and reading with her children bring her joy. She finds crocheting amigurumi, and folding origami fascinating.

Oh, and there is always time for afternoon tea!

Website: https://springbrookorbillabong.wordpress.com

Instagram: https://instagram.com/alexa_jaye241

Chapter 3

Being an Expat Parent
Sangeetha Narayan

It is said that being a parent is akin to rebirth.

In those three minutes that it takes to know that a new being is entering the family, life as we know it completely changes. The fact that we are in an alien country and starting from scratch just adds a whole new dimension to the situation.

I consider myself to be lucky as I had four whole years to adjust to another country. However, the truth is that I truly adjusted in my adopted country only after my daughter was born.

When we first moved, I was an introvert, and I missed my home country. I did not feel comfortable driving, which made me dependent on my husband for transport. I was a homemaker and didn't have the drive or necessity to interact with different people. My life revolved around my home. It was not until I was expecting my first child that I ventured out of my safety net. I had to step out of the house more often. I had to go for all doctor appointments. That was when I truly saw the people in this alien country. I noticed the smiling faces, other expecting families, doctors, nurses, etc. I found that other than the color of our skin, there was not much of a difference between the people of my birth country, India and the people of my adopted country, The United States of America. At the doctor's office, we were all parents concerned about the welfare of our child, and we were all given the same degree of importance by every professional. If an expectant woman groaned in discomfort, all of us felt it and sympathized.

We were all in the same boat and that was a common bond!

Days turned into months and it was time for my daughter to be born. My parents were supposed to come to help with the baby but they couldn't make it before the delivery. My daughter was born way before her due date and sabotaged all our careful planning.

A struggle most expat parents experience...being alone and wanting your mom during the most important time of rebirth with a child.

When my mom expressed her guilt for not being able to be present at the time of my delivery, I reassured her and myself, *"Even if you had been present, you could not have helped me in the way that the professionals at the hospital did."*

Whether it was scheduling my appointments, checking to make sure everything was fine with my baby, at the time of her birth or the checkups after, I have dealt with people of all different cultures and countries.

Nobody stopped to check my background, nor did I feel the need to check where they came from.

A year later, when my daughter had her first wheezing attack, we rushed her to emergency care. We were taken under the wings of the doctors and nurses in that hospital. I will forever be grateful for the expert care and concern that my daughter received during those agonizing days.

When my daughter was extremely sick, I sat next to her and recited the Hanuman Chalisa, an Indian prayer song. During their routine visit, one of the on-call doctors asked me what I was singing. When I told him it was a prayer, he said, *"That felt so wonderful to hear. It even calmed me down and I'm sure your daughter must be feeling relaxed too."* It was a small gesture and yet stays with me to this day.

I realized then that there were certain things in life like music & faith, that know no barriers.

That day, I felt connected to another human being, just as he was connected to me and my child. Being an expat parent has taught me that we are all just human beings, nothing more, nothing less.

Emotions Beyond Color

Deep down, beneath all the black, brown, and white that we see, people are just a bundle of emotions; happy, sad, angry, depressed or stressed. How they appear externally has nothing to do with what they are feeling inside. That makes sense as we don't go around declaring problems that we are facing. We put on a smile and cover our tears. Everyone does that!

Reaching Out Can Make a Difference

Reaching out to people can sometimes be as easy as smiling and saying a cheerful, "Hello!" We never know who needs just that to make their day better. Maybe when stepping outside to drop our child at the bus stop, at the store or just waving at someone, can make us feel seen. **When we follow our instinct of spreading joy, some of it is bound to sprinkle back on us.**

Thread of Commonality

Surrounding ourselves with people who share some common bond with us, like maybe having children of the same age group, will only strengthen relationships. It makes sense to hang on to them and keep adding more to this tribe. And if the tribe has people from different cultures, it makes it more interesting. It promotes cultural exchange and encourages our children to branch out in their own friendships.

Share Your Roots

This whole multicultural approach only works if we have something to offer. When we respect our roots, we will find that people seek us more. Every country comes with its own cultural heritage and values. To lift up someone, we do not have to put ourselves down. **The higher we stand, the higher we can lift others.**

Accept the good with the not-so-good

If we can accept ourselves, mistakes, and all, we definitely can accept other people with their faults. When our children watch us and understand that mistakes can be forgiven, they will learn to accept their own mistakes.

"When you move from one country to another, you have to accept that there are some things that are better and some things that are worse, and there is nothing you can do about it." - Bill Bryson, a traveler, and an American author.

So, the choice is ours, whether we choose to harp on about the not-so-good or accept it and look at the brighter side of living an expat life. With the right kind of glasses, we can see an amazing balance that life offers, even in a foreign country.

ABOUT SANGEETHA NARAYAN

Sangeetha Narayan is a freelance writer residing in Ellicott City, MD with her husband and two children. A stay-at-home-mom, volunteer in her children's school, freelance writer at raising world children, and a book reviewer at an online book club, she loves to don many hats at one time. She has also been published on Women's Era and Dimdima. Sangeetha Narayan practices what she likes to call spiritual parenting and encourages other parents to be aware of their thoughts using her writing.

Website: https://sursangeet2000.wordpress.com/

Social media: https://www.facebook.com/sangreads/

Chapter 4

Struggles of Expat Life
Madhu Challa

"Maybe you had to leave to really miss a place;
maybe you had to travel to figure out how
beloved your starting point was."
— *Jodi Picoult, Handle with Care*

There I was bidding farewell to my parents and my younger brother, taking my first ever international flight alone, for my Master's program in the United States of America. Land of dreams and unlimited possibilities. It was kind of crazy because I had never traveled alone. And here I was, moving to a new country in an entirely different continent. It was mind-boggling! I often wonder how I managed it all.

Those first indispensable days still afresh in my memory are the hardest and undeniably life changing. Challenges came calling! My English-speaking skills became a barrier. It was challenging to have conversations with the bank representatives, school admissions staff, or even my professors. I always hesitated.

I would tag along with my friends to apply for students' jobs. I got away without talking much for some time. But soon, I realized that my friends were uncomfortable with me tagging along since we were applying for the same job.

I had to tell myself to give up hiding and face my fears - "the only way to get through it is to go through it."

So, I went around looking for jobs and finally landed one, as a custodian. Back in India, I did basic chores at home, but this was something else. I began to regret leaving my family, friends, and everything behind. I had to swallow my pride and get with the program. The experience turned out to be one of my biggest lessons. I learned to be humble and be appreciative of every opportunity and challenge that life threw at me. **Contributing to the community and the land is critical no matter what kind of job you are doing, if you are happy doing it.**

I am thankful that I already had a community and student support group. Living in a country with an unfamiliar language can easily find the most straightforward things considerably more complicated. Asking for information, buying the food you want, transportation, or finding medicine in a pharmacy, all these simple tasks suddenly become daunting.

It is not the big things, but the small unknown things that you come across are super challenging. Knowing that *"Freeway is Highway"* and just because *"someone is smiling does not mean they are friendly"* helped me better navigate my day to day life with ease.

"Little things seem nothing, but they give peace, like those meadow flowers which individually seem odorless but altogether perfume the air." - Georges Bernanos

Soon I graduated and started working. Initial conversations with my managers were unnerving. Being raised to listen and follow is the norm in India. So obviously I brought that mindset to my work. I never dared to bring up issues and shied away from many opportunities that came along, where I was required to speak up and present. This, as you might expect only hindered my professional growth. Thanks to an opportunity, I had no other choice but to give a talk on a particular topic. The presentation went very well, and suddenly, I was not afraid anymore! I started wondering why did it take me such a long time to get over this fear? I told myself that I needed to be bold. All these years, I was standing in my own way, while it took only one initiative for my whole perspective to change.

Fast forward a few years, I had two kids, and I became a stay-at-home mom. Even though my kids were born in the USA, I still faced the same challenges as other new immigrant parents. I wanted my kids to understand and embrace both cultures; The one they are growing up in and the one which their parents grew up with. So, what was the outcome? Confusion on both sides! No wonder why our kids are called ABCD - 'American Born Confused Desi'.

Most parents face a multitude of challenges to raise their kids in a different culture. They are in a constant race to overcome their fears and difficulties. Most importantly, the critical problem I saw was the loss of identity.

The key to unlocking our *"loss of identity"* is learning to see ourselves differently. We all try to fit in and hardly realize that we are, in fact, supposed to stand out.

Being comfortable and confident in our skin and standing our ground are essential tools that we can arm ourselves and our kids with, no matter what the situation.

These days we can find anything and everything we need to teach our kids about our culture and heritage. We can also find many parents taking fantastic initiatives to launch products like books, games, and toys that teach kids about their roots and heritage. While all these are amazing, what is more important is the effort.

There is no other better way than taking our kids to the place that we, their parents, were born and raised in. They will learn much more by going to places and interacting with people of a different culture.

As Wendell Berry said, *"Nobody can discover the world for someone else. Only when we discover it for ourselves does it become common ground and a common bond, and we cease to be alone."*

Despite all the difficulties and the hard times, we've been through in our expat/immigrant journey, we may feel that we wouldn't want it any other way.

"I may not have gone where I intended to go, but I think I have ended up where I needed to be." - Douglas Adams.

Settling abroad fills you with confidence and a great sense of achievement; it makes us more adaptable and stronger towards change and future challenges. Our journey can be less stressful and more enjoyable if we -

Ask for Help

Ask for help! People will help you if you ask. Leave your shyness at bay. Just like, getting better at a sport or public speaking, you must practice, and you have to do things that make you a little uncomfortable. You can gain confidence through experience and by putting yourself out there.

Mingle All the Way

How many of us try to learn about different cultures and languages? Learn before you move and continue to learn. Talk to different people. Once you are in a new country, invite others to understand your culture and visit them. Make the connection! Move in and out of your community circles. **It is essential to immerse yourself in the culture you are living in. You cannot do this if you socialize only with your cultural conglomerate.**

Be Open

Once you have left your home country, you start missing things in a way you probably did not expect. Food is usually one of these things. Finding your favorite food made to your taste is almost impossible. So, it can be the strangest little things that you miss, when you live abroad. It may be a television program in your regional language or a place you miss visiting to unwind. In the end, it becomes a matter of trying something new and learning to love other things like the local cuisine.

A Language is But a Vehicle

One of the most challenging parts of a move would be to speak and understand the expat country's language. Learn. Take classes, observe. One day, I had this "Aha!" moment, when I read a book from a renowned author who once told, *"A language is but a vehicle. It is the person inside who is weaving the story, and that's more important. So, get on with your story, and the language will fall into place".*

We all have a story to tell and share. Don't let these minor hurdles set you back.

All in all, what brings humanity together is that we try to co-exist amidst a myriad of differences; we dare, we succeed. When we self-reflect, it boils down to a similar sentiment when looked at from the other end of the lens.

Slowly but surely, we will find our peace. It's the magic of human energy. We are one soul, all working together in a singular momentum to build better lives.

ABOUT MADHU CHALLA

Madhu is the Founder and CEO of Pretty Pokets, a Designer Bags and Accessories Company for Women. She has a master's degree in Electrical Engineering and was a Hardware Engineer at Intel Corp for 10 Years. Madhu is a doting mom of two and loves to start her day with a soul pleasing half a cup of Indian coffee and an inspirational book.

Website: https://prettypokets.com

Instagram: https://instagram.com/prettypokets

Chapter 5

Being Seen Differently
Minali Bajaj - Syed

Many of us have the wonderful opportunity to interact with people from various spectrums of life - who look, talk, dress, eat and behave very differently from us. We see each other differently.

To see people for who they are: with all their beautifully unique features, wonderful languages, and culturally rich ethnic backgrounds, without any prejudice or bias, is what makes us share the commonality of being global citizens.

I was born and raised in Kuwait, but by nationality, I am an Indian. That is because the State of Kuwait does not give citizenship to those born there. Yet, home to me will always be Kuwait! **Home is where our belongingness lies: our family, our friends, our childhood, days spent laughing and nights spent crying; Home truly is where the heart has memories etched!**

In the summer of 2000, I moved to the US to pursue my University education. Being far from home was hard but settling in was an absolute culture shock. As I began to make friends and mingle with my roommates, I realized that even though we were all from different parts of the world, we were in the same boat: away from our family. We all looked different, dressed differently, and spoke different languages, but bonded over so many common struggles like settling into a new place, missing home-cooked meals and not having family around.

Interestingly, most of the friends I made were Hispanics, African Americans and a few Indian-Americans. It was not easy making friends with white/Caucasian people. Conversations with them never extended beyond the classroom. Whereas friendships with International students and so called 'people-of-color', started in the classrooms and went all the way to hanging out together for lunch, at the library, at the mall and more. Their level of acceptance was humbling, as they made me feel like one of their own.

It was surprising though that fostering a friendship with Indian students, who had come from India, was equally hard. Once, one of the Indian students asked me, *"You have come from Dubai right?"* and on another occasion, I was asked by another Indian student, *"Why did you move from London to the US?"* Probably because my English sounded different, and I did not have an 'Indian' accent, it was assumed that I was from London or the Gulf (read: Dubai).

This is when I realized that they never saw me as one of their own because they knew I had not come from India. This experience taught me one especially important lesson: never have preconceived notions about anyone!

The Indian students from India thought that I did not have an 'Indian' accent; my American friends thought that I had a 'slight accent'; and my lovely Hispanic friends never even addressed this because they knew that having a thick 'Hispanic' accent is part of their being. Try saying *"paella"* or *"vanilla"* in Spanish; you'll know what I mean!

On the positive side of that, not being seen by Indians as 'one of their own' made me befriend others from diverse backgrounds. I had friends from countries, which I never knew existed! This is when I learned the importance and value of diversity. It introduces the world to you and opens your mind and vision to places you have never been.

Even though being in a clique seems comfortable and convenient, it does not help one grow or learn more.

Upon completing my education, I moved back to Kuwait. I missed being around a diverse set of people. I left a job within the first week because I just could not see myself among one set of people, who viewed me as an outsider. Then eventually, I got a job with an American retail brand. I even got my driver's license easily upon showing my US driver's license.

Once again, I was seen differently in a different place. This time around, as an 'American Return!'

My workplace had a wonderfully diverse environment. And this was a huge reason why my job never felt like work. It felt like an extension of my University life. The only thing different was now I did not have to take any exams!

The world has moved at an amazingly fast pace since the year 2000. With huge technological advances, the world is smaller than ever before. Yet, one thing that unfortunately still exists is the stereotyping of people.

Even today, when we go to a restaurant, we are handed menus in Arabic. Upon requesting menus in English, we are sometimes told that we look Kuwaiti or Persian, but not Indians.

I can never forget an instance when a restaurant server of far-eastern descent told me that I didn't look Indian because I was relatively light-skinned. I had to politely school the lady about how big and spread-out India is; and how people from different races and descents settled in different parts of India. In addition to this, I also educated her about the fact that the closer a place is to the equator, the darker the skin tone of the people is, due to the intensity of the sunlight.

Our skin tone is just a shade on a spectrum of colors. We need to stop using skin color, language, physical features and mannerisms as a tool for stereotyping ethnicity. We should start seeing people for who they are; and not how different they are from us.

The one thing I've made sure to pass down to my children is inclusion. We have always encouraged them to make friends from different cultures and backgrounds. The school they were enrolled in had children from so many different nationalities – Indians, Kuwaitis, Filipinos, Lebanese, Jordanians, Pakistanis, Bangladeshis, Africans and more. Today, they have respect and acceptance for all and even learn a thing or two from their friends about their countries' and cultures'.

Even when it comes to socializing, I see that my children are happier among people who speak various languages and who are from different parts of the world. Their curiosity comes out of the bag and it gives rise to conversations that go beyond borders. They always want to explore and learn more about the world.

This global mindset helps them, especially, during travel as they never feel out of place and it is easier for them to blend in.

Stereotyping people or viewing them as different from us, will take us towards segregation. To create and become Global Citizens, we should steer away from segregation, and move towards integration and eventually inclusion.

Whereas being comfortable in our cliques will lead to making our future generation live in isolation.

Even if we are viewed differently, we must make the effort to connect with each other on a humane level and appreciate each other's ways of life.

One of the best places to acquaint yourselves with people from different cultures is while you are in transit at the airport. Try it!

31

When in transit, give your book or phone a miss, and start observing around to see how beautifully diverse God has made his creations.

As said by Mahatma Gandhi, *"Our ability to reach unity in diversity will be the beauty and the test of our civilization."*

ABOUT MINALI BAJAJ-SYED

Minali Bajaj-Syed is the Managing Editor at Raising World Children LLC

She is an Indian, born and settled in Kuwait. Having lived in Kuwait, India and the United States, she has had the wonderful opportunity to experience a diverse set of cultures.

Minali has a double degree in Arts and Education. Currently a homeschooling mom; she is a passionate mother of two kids. She is constantly learning, evolving and trying to spread some positivity. Minali believes that being content and grateful to God is the key to happiness in life. She hopes to bring a change of heart and provoke the mind, through her writing.

Cooking scrumptious meals and baking desserts is an absolute stressbuster for Minali. She looks forward to sharing her quick and easy recipes with others around the world, through her Instagram handle - Cinnamon_Cardamom

Instagram: https://instagram.com/cinnamon_cardamom

Website: https://raisingworldchildren.com/minali/

Chapter 6

Moving Back to Native Country
Sindhuja Kumar

As a Third Culture Kid, my life was always an emotional rollercoaster.

Third culture kids (TCK) are individuals who are (or were as children) raised in a culture other than their parents' or the **culture** of their country of nationality and live in a different environment during a significant part of their child development years.

Slightly different than many since my relocations were only within my country. To understand me saying this, one needs to understand that India has multitudes of subcultures in every city and state. Thus, moving often, while exciting, it also felt connectionless. People who often relocate will relate. It never gets easy.

My family moved around a fair amount because of my mom's government job; meaning we lived in a lot of cities for a few years at a time. Every time we moved, I felt uprooted.

I had to often give painstaking attention to my new surroundings and put-up barriers. I was always the new girl and it was hard for me as I hated the attention. By the time I began to adapt and finally settle in, my mom would tell me we were moving again. Depressed, I hated the helplessness.

There were some silver linings, such as developing coping skills and doing really well academically due to the exposure I got.

College life brought some stability as I took up residential college.

When I got married, my husband had to move to the USA for work. I realized my life with the packers and movers is intertwined, and even I cannot untangle it. Leaving my community behind was tough, especially when I was in an arranged marriage. It was like starting from scratch, without any support. My entire childhood flashed before my eyes!

I gradually began to love my expat life in the USA, although we also moved a fair amount between states. I was inspired by the melting pot lifestyle of people in the USA, who came together from different cultures and blended in so well.

People from all over the world - tourists, immigrants, green card holders and more were visiting, living here and sharing ideas to create a new culture.

I loved my independence! I got to decide where to go and what to feed my family. My formative years' experience prevented me from getting into culture shock. To the contrary, I was opened to adapt.

Once my daughter was born, she too had a great life experience in the USA with exposure to a high-end lifestyle compared to India. But unfortunately, just as we were settling into our fourth home, we had to make a life-changing decision to move back to India.

My husband's parents were getting older and frailer. They needed help, and it was now up to us to support them. I found myself packing again!

Adapting to the Idea of moving back

While India was my home, I had mixed feelings about going back. I was ready for the move, but I knew how difficult this move could be for my daughter, who was just a few years old.

I did not let my insecurities cloud my judgement, focusing instead on the positive aspects. I tried to make this transition as smooth as possible. A few things helped me make this move easier for us. The most important of those was communication.

"Courage is knowing what not to fear." - Plato

I believe, as parents we should teach our kids to truly understand their abilities and knowledge, so they can no longer fear the unknown. The courage gained helps them steer through every situation.

Adapting to our home culture as a family

I tried extremely hard to prepare my daughter for the change because of the vast difference in the way of life in India and the USA. It was still tricky. I feared that she might face a cultural identity crisis. To make the transition easier, I took a job as a nursery teacher at the same preschool she was admitted in.

Because I was close by, I could help her through cultural differences, a new schooling system and even different washrooms. Yes, in India, the bathrooms are different from those in the USA; and for my daughter, there was suddenly a whole new plumbing system to deal with, including a wet floor.

I was so glad I was there for her to help her through these differences. One might find this silly, but even mosquitos were a struggle. My daughter had a hypersensitive reaction to their bites. Being mentally prepared as a family helped a lot.

Familial Support

My in-laws gave me good guidance on raising my child. They helped in more ways than I could possibly imagine - from the time of her birth in India, via long-distance voice and video calls, and then immeasurably when we returned to India. I could not be more grateful to them for the physical and mental support.

It was so good to be close to family again! They not only cooked for us and helped us settle in, but they also gave us great advice regarding doctors and hospitals as well. India has an excellent health care system, but it is vastly different from the USA.

Open Communication with my Daughter

I remembered how my parents were remiss to explain to me why we were moving or what it meant. I was determined to make my kid understand what was ahead of her. I made it honest & positive. I acknowledged her feelings and allowed her to grieve. I did not gloss over anything, but I did explain how lovely it would be, being back in India with family. I also explained that she would make new friends in India, her cousins would be close by, and of course, she could always stay in touch with her old friends in the USA.

When you are young, and you must move places, you feel like the world is ending!

Whenever my kid was sad, I initiated a conversation with her, and I made sure to listen to her.

I understood the importance of listening, and I never brushed her feelings away. When it was time to leave, I made sure that she said a proper goodbye to her friends and her favorite teachers. That was an essential part of closure.

Giving a heads up on what to expect in the new community can prevent them from feeling alienated. I told her about the park close to the new home, and I gave her a description of her new school.

I showed her pictures on the internet of where we were going, so she would have an image in her head to look forward to.

I assured her that we would bring with us all the things that were dear to her. There was no way we would leave her favorite teddy bear behind or her favorite pink dress. I understood the importance of familiarity of her favorite belongings.

Give Kids Time for Friendships

After moving to a new home, kids can't just go out and make friends. They need some time to settle in, so until then, give them space. Do not force them to initiate conversation; instead, you can start the conversation with your community people. I reached out to our neighbors and their kids and found connections with kids from the same school.

Teaching your child social skills will help them quickly make new friends and connect with new classmates.

Connect with Old Friends

Keep in touch with your kid's best friends from the former school through phone, video calls, Facebook messenger or occasional vacation meetups. If your kid is very tiny, make sure you get your preschool teacher's number. My daughter always wanted to talk to her teacher or show her when she has done or achieved something. We are still in touch and it means a lot to her.

Allow Frustration & Questions

One must not clam up when your kid asks questions about the move and new surroundings. It develops the trust they have for you, which will be helpful in the upcoming edgy days of adjustments.

Let them know that you understand their grief about leaving behind their friends. Acknowledge their negative feelings. Give them assurance that everything will be alright, and a little patience would make things fall into place eventually. Let them know that you are there for them.

Build the Excitement of Moving Gradually

It takes time for "anxiousness of moving" to change into "excitement of moving", particularly for a kid. So, do not expect a change overnight. Try to create a sense of adventure. Read some books that talk about inspiring travel and amazing adventures of travel within your native country. Assist your child to create plans for the move. Have them make to-do lists of tasks unique to them. I gave my kid a small trolley and asked her to pack it with her favorite things that she didn't want to leave behind.

Be a Community Builder

Younger kids are more like mirrors, and they almost always reflect our behavior. When they realize that their parents are happy, they can sense the vibe.

So become a part of the community yourself. Try to meet new people through local events, schools, groups, or organizations. Reach out to people who have kids the same age as your child. Invite them over for lunch or even for tea, to make it easier for your child to meet other children.

My daughter cried when we had to give some of her toys away. But gradually she understood and started packing her things along with us. We made her accountable for choosing the toys that she wanted to donate to goodwill and the toys she wanted to take back to India.

Deciding authority gives children a sense of responsibility, giving them the power to make decisions on what they want to share and what they want to hold on to.

I am so glad we returned home, and it was the best decision we took for our family. I do understand that it can feel frightening, when you go through the process of moving, but take it from my experience - a little preparation will make it an adventure of a lifetime!

ABOUT SINDHUJA KUMAR

Sindhuja Kumar is a software engineer, freelance writer, digital illustrator, early childhood educator, based in Bangalore. She is also the founder of playdokids.com. She has combined her education, teaching experience and parenting experience to create Playdokids. It is a discover & book platform, which connects parents with non-academic kids' activity providers in India. An amazing resource, this platform opens up a world of opportunities for parents to identify their kid's personality and discover relevant activities, classes and events for kids. A passionate mother, multipotentialite with a flair for the creative arts and technology, Sindhuja believes that by identifying a child's unique temperament and personality, parents can help children become more resilient in our unpredictable world.

Website : https://playdokids.com/

Instagram: https://www.instagram.com/playdokids/

Chapter 7

Being Multicultural When Your Community is Monocultural
Maureen Argon

"In the end,
we will conserve only what we love,
we will love only what we understand,
and we will understand
only what we are taught."
— Baba Dioum

Growing up, I thought my family was the only immigrant family in our small suburban town of Greenfield Park, across the St. Lawrence River from Montreal. To my child-mind everyone was English. I spoke English, but that was not my native language, nor my culture. My parents emigrated from Europe just after WWII. My mom was German, and my dad was Russian - Soviet in fact and we spoke German at home.

The experience of that war was still very real for most. Everyone had been touched by it. During my childhood in the 1960's, Hollywood made a lot of war movies, feeding on personal memories. And I guess the stereotypes penetrated the imagination, becoming real.

I remember a morning in the school yard waiting for the bell - a group of my fellow grade school classmates encircled me, taunting me and yelling *"Heil Hitler!"* I clutched my little blue school bag and started spinning, my arm outstretched, swatting those yelling kids with my school bag with all my might!

That day, I learned shame for my heritage. I never saw myself reflected in my community and I didn't know where I fit in. It affected my confidence and made me afraid. **Fear is a perfect partner to shame, unworthiness, domination, objectification, and it is often expressed as violence, power and suppression. It makes us live a small half-life.**

Fast forward a few decades: I've lived in Canada's three largest cities, all very multicultural and diverse and I've witnessed many waves of cultural migration. Home today, and where I raised my two children, is a small rural town in conservative Ontario. Many residents here can trace their family roots back almost 200 years. It's a beautiful community and the people are good but there's not a lot of diversity here.

It's important that my children understand not only their own cultural heritage but also appreciate that people come in all different shapes, colors and sizes, speak different languages and have different ways of dressing, eating and worship. And most importantly, this adds richness to our life. But how do I do that?

"You either walk inside your story and own it, or you stand outside your story and hustle for your worthiness." - Brené Brown

To appreciate anyone else, we must first appreciate ourselves and where we come from. This is equally important for a child as it is for an adult. In fact, I am going to come right out and say that if we raise our children to truly appreciate themselves, they will grow up to be confident, secure adults.

Unless we do the inner work, we are never going to feel fully worthy of our place in any community or in the world. Nothing

we do externally, will make up for that. If you do not feel your own self-worth, you cannot fully see anyone else's.

So, you may be wondering, "what the heck does this have to do with raising your child to see beyond their own experience, to embrace kids from other cultures and traditions, instead of pointing a finger."

To raise a child - a human who sees (really sees) another human - not a skin color; not a lunch box filled with weird stuff that smells funny (like my liverwurst sandwiches on rye plus the dill pickle my mom packed for my lunch); not a kid speaking with an accent, who doesn't know how to play the school yard games. It all comes down to this - you can't give what you don't have!

The path to recognizing that we are more similar than different, is self-worth. Self-worth is essential to feeling safe and secure and knowing you belong.

When my son was pre-school aged, we would go to the park regularly - sand bucket, shovel, and back-end loader in hand. Often, he would share with other children but sometimes he didn't want to and that was ok with me. I would never force him. I had read somewhere that when you gave your child permission to not share their toys, it encouraged them to be more generous. Why? Because they developed a stronger sense of security.

And I believe the same thing happens with concepts like being curious about people, culture and developing a sense of inclusivity. It must begin with feeling secure, the very opposite of fearfulness.

So ultimately, it does not matter if you live in a diverse community or not. With a secure sense of self, which grows as the child does, your child will have a spirit that is open, curious, welcoming, ready and receptive. Then, share all the resources available to show your child the wonderful diversity of the world - books, music, art, museums, food and more.

Here are some tips to help your children feel open-to and at-home, with cultural diversity:

Treat Your Children with Respect

Children are no less entitled to it than adults. Speak kindly to your children. Understand that they have different likes or dislikes than you. Acknowledge their developmental stages and what they're capable of. At the back of my mind, I think about being old and not able to do things for myself. And I hope my children will be patient and loving with me. I would not want to be yelled at because I can't tie my shoes fast enough!

Help your Children Feel Confident and Worthy

A confident person who knows they are worthy is an open person. They are not fearful; they have a strong sense of self. The more fearful a child is, the more they are likely to grow up living a small life, imprisoned by their own fear of what is not familiar.

A few ways to help your child develop confidence and a strong sense of self -

1. Allow them to say "no". This helps them create and express their boundaries.

2. Try "Choice Theory Parenting". This method of conflict resolution allows parents to eliminate arguments with their child about compliance, while encouraging their child to develop important skills. You as a parent choose the choices for your child. Let's say they are misbehaving in a restaurant. You offer them the choice of behaving properly or leaving and they decide.

3. Engage your child in conversation and ask them what they think. Let them know their opinion matters.

Listen to World Music

Sure, your child loves The Wheels On The Bus and it's easy to put that on to keep them occupied and entertained when you're in the car or trying to cook dinner. But do not underestimate your child's ability to absorb, appreciate and enjoy music that is not what we typically think of as children's music. The brain of a young child is so plastic that it's not unusual for a 5-year-old to be able to speak several languages if they are exposed to them. Everybody enjoys music and rhythm. Rhythm and melody are ancient ways of storytelling. It is part of every culture. The more our children are exposed to different things the more familiar they become.

Explore different neighborhoods in your city or take a day trip to a larger center if your community is small.

Our family would often drive to our nearest city, Toronto (population: 3 million) and just walk around. The diverse population, the languages we heard, the feast for the eye in the clothing people wore was just not something we had in our small community. The more you do this, the more your children and you, see that people are so beautifully diverse.

And a few more tips from Homa Sabet Tavangar, author of "Growing Up Global: Raising Children to be at Home in the World" (Ballantine). -

- Take the kids to foreign films

- Sample ethnic restaurants

- Put a world map on the wall, with a thumbtack on every country the kids learn about

- Help your children's teachers make global classrooms

- Encourage the kids to invite friends from other cultures to dinner

- If your native tongue is not English, use it with your children

At the heart, if we hope to create a world where we respect each other, where we are inclusive, where we live in peace with each other, where we have harmony between communities and nations - a world that is our global home - then we must recognize our own worthiness.

And if I am worthy, then you are worthy!

ABOUT MAUREEN ARGON

Maureen is a former national radio producer and journalist with CBC Radio. She's also a freelance writer and an Award-Winning Editor focusing on stories in the arts and current affairs. Maureen is a foodie and nutrition nerd, who has led culinary walking tours in Stratford Ontario, her hometown, gaining the attention of the New York Times. Today, she is the founder of Healthier + Happier for Life, a coaching business that helps women and men improve their nutrition and health so they can meet and beat the challenges of a busy and productive life. Maureen's greatest joy was becoming a mom later in life. Her favourite thing in the world is hanging out with her son Nikolai and her daughter Clare.

LinkedIn : https://www.linkedin.com/in/maureenargon/

Instagram : https://www.instagram.com/maureenargon/

Chapter 8

Moving to a New City
Rivkah Krisnoff

*"It's different cultures that make
the world go round at the end of the day."
- Samantha Fox, English singer, songwriter,
actress, and former glamour model*

In the mid-seventies, we moved from Dublin, Ireland to the small village town of Nsukka, Nigeria, home to the University of Nigeria, where my father would be teaching Physics for the next 15 years. Prior to this, he was a substitute professor for 2 years at Trinity College, Ireland's oldest university.

The Nigerian government brought in Indian professors to teach at the University of Nigeria. My father ended up there because his position at Trinity College, Dublin had come to an abrupt halt. Going back to Bangladesh was not an option. After all, how can an atheist survive in a predominantly Muslim country? He was a non-conformist, who felt very isolated within his large family. On Friday afternoons, while most men prayed at the mosque, my father remained behind at home. It was hard to be different.

My father had a very rough childhood, having lost his mother to typhus fever as a young child. My grandfather was married 3 times. One of his wives had severe mental issues that required her to be institutionalized. It was this woman who verbally abused my father, constantly mocking him for being so studious. Ironically, my father eventually saw education as the only way to escape from his unhappy life.

He escaped by studying for his PhD in Glasgow (Scotland), and then teaching in Durham (England), Syracuse (NY), Dhaka (Bangladesh), Dublin (Ireland), Trieste (Italy), Nsukka (Nigeria), Newark (Delaware).

Hence, my childhood was defined by constantly moving to a different city across different countries.

Growing up moving from city to city, we found other Bengali families and became a part of that community. Dublin, Ireland was the only exception. I managed to find friends, even becoming the popular girl in my class, while my parents still remained isolated.

In Nsukka, Nigeria things were different. Within a few days of moving into the university guest hostel, a Bengali family came to visit us to welcome us to the small Bengali community. Not including us, there were a total of 5 Bengali families in Nsukka. There were also Hindu and 2 Sikh families, totaling almost 20. Every male head was either a university professor teaching Physics, Chemistry, Math, Biology, Geology, Philosophy, Engineering, or a variety of other subjects. The wives did all the cooking and cleaning with the help of servants. All the children either went to the primary school located inside the campus or the boys and girls' secondary school a few miles outside the campus.

Life in Nsukka was very tranquil. It was a small town with a local marketplace – no malls, no restaurants, no McDonalds, no movie theaters. Our entertainment was either watching VHS videos with British, American, Hindi, or Bengali movies, or dinner parties. The kids played with each other. Either we played games and toys that our parents bought overseas, or we played house, cops and robbers, and other games we made up.

Given that there were very few Bengali girls my age, I spent most of my time between the ages of 13 and 16, reading novels and preparing for my O-Levels. During my teenage years, my Nigerian counterparts were in boarding school. I was a day student, which meant that after school was over, my father picked me up and took me home at the sequestered University campus, nestled in the valley.

Inside the campus, all faculty members and their families lived in university provided housing - a one story bungalow with three bedrooms, a sitting and dining room, a kitchen, an attached one-car garage, as well as a front and back porch. We all had a large front and back yard with red sandy soil.

The Bengali families mixed with each other and not the Hindu or Sikh families. None of the Indian families socialized with the Nigerians.

We had no idea what the Nigerian culture was like. The part of Nigeria we lived in were Christians, mostly Catholics. The only interactions we had with Nigerians were the servants, vendors at the local market, or for the Indian subcontinent men, their fellow Nigerian professors, and department heads. Our knowledge of Nigerians was limited to awareness of their religion, the language they spoke (Igbo, Yoruba, and Hausa) and the foods they ate - yams, cassava, egusi soup (vegetables and meat mixture). At home we ate the usual Indian dishes - rice, curried beef/chicken, fish cooked in masala, and curried vegetables.

Our social life consisted of visiting each other's homes during the late afternoons or after dinner. We also had dinner parties, where we ate biryani and other fancy Indian dishes. These dinner parties involved conversations or watching videos.

Our family was the exception, where we had Bengali and Indian friends. One of my parent's friends was a Nigerian man married to a Russian woman, which I found fascinating. Another family was a Nigerian married to a British lady with 4 children.

Although the dinner parties were alcohol free, there were a few Indian families who indulged in alcohol parties. Even though we were not practicing Muslims, my mother disliked alcohol. As a teenager, I found the alcohol parties most entertaining because conversations tended to be lively and boisterous.

Such was life in tranquil Nsukka. When it was Eid, we celebrated it with the other Bengali families. There were no Indian or Bengali stores to buy saris, salwar kameez, kurta etc. Only when traveling to our native countries during the summer holidays could we purchase traditional clothes and spices.

Growing up in Nigeria, England, Ireland, and the United States, I learned that moving from city to city, you inevitably found other Bengali families, except in Ireland in the 1970s. We were a subculture within the culture of the country we lived in - eating the same foods of our home country, watching Bengali videos, speaking our native tongue, and celebrating the religious holidays. I always felt so sad that we were such an isolated community, never mingling with others outside our culture. I felt that it was being rude to the host country.

Such was my life in Nsukka, Nigeria. It was surreal, living in post-colonial Nigeria. Like the Indian subcontinent, Nigeria was under British rule. The elementary and secondary schools my brother and I attended were run by the British system. I spelt "colour" the Queen's English way. I studied for my O-Levels on my own, which I took at the British consulate in Nigeria. Ordinary or O-Levels are subject based exams one takes at the age of 16. Passing these exams in English, Math, the Sciences, a second language (usually French), history, geography and economics meant you were qualified to take the Advanced Levels (A-Levels) to attend a British university.

I was lonely and culturally confused – a British Born Confused Desi living in sleepy Nsukka. Often, I asked myself how we ended up in Nigeria? A Bengali family in Nsukka, Nigeria of all places!

My childhood experiences moving from city to city and country to country taught me flexibility. Life is a constant adjustment to changing circumstances.

For instance, I dreamed of carving a lucrative work-at-home marketing career at IBM so that I could have a baby and enjoy the company benefits. Upper management had other plans, and I got laid off.

International travel taught me the importance of adapting and creating a new vision.

I could have succumbed to depression and settled for a lower paying job. Instead I created a new dream - entrepreneurship.

The other lesson I learned is that true growth is expanding your horizons to meet different people across different cultures. Imagine if Asian-Americans, African Americans, Anglo-Americans, Hispanics, etc. co-mingled without losing our identities. We would be that much closer to a post racial country.

Most important of all, the legacy we would leave our children is that of a multicultural society.

ABOUT RIVKAH KRISNOFF

Irene Rivkah Krasnoff lives in Dallas, Texas with her husband Neil and her 8-year-old daughter Bracha. She is a British-born American-Bengali Desi who converted to Judaism. Thanks to an ambitious father, who was a Physics professor with a passion for experiencing different countries, Irene Rivkah Krasnoff was born in Scotland, and grew up in England, Ireland, Bangladesh, Nigeria and the United States. Going to primary and secondary school in Bangladesh, Ireland, Nigeria and England taught her to accept people for who they are and not to judge them based on the color of their skin.

Website: https://www.sapirmanagementgroupllc.com/

Instagram: Instagram.com/digital_mom_entrepreneur/

Chapter 9

Displacement by War
Aditi Wardhan Singh

"War is delightful to those who have no experience of it."
- Desiderius Erasmus

"Where are you from?" when people who look like you, ask an impressionable mind, is when one knows you probably do not belong. I was 10 when this first happened, after the 1990 Gulf War.

The world fears war and yet encourages it, in a million small ways. By encouraging divisiveness, judgement, thoughtless comments, and blind sharing of content.

Many do not think of the consequences it has, in the biggest of ways to the smallest. The colossal wave each ripple creates.

Everyone I know gets very fascinated to learn that I was in Kuwait during the Gulf War. They cannot wait to get the juicy details.

I share about the experience too. How my dad stocked up with weeks of food supplies in a day. How mom filled every empty vessel in the house with water fearing water contamination. How the Iraqis behaved with Indians and Kuwaitis differently. How we taped the windows shut with garbage bags fearing chemical bombing. How I felt when bombs went around our home. How we managed to escape on one of the first flights out, during the height of the invasion.

How my mom packed up suitcases full of stuff she hoped we would take to India with us. How still we ended up fleeing; my mom and me with a 6-month baby and a bag of diapers and jewelry sown in her petticoat. How we left *everything* we owned behind.

What it was like to go back to an empty apartment two years later, devoid of all our treasured possessions.

Interestingly, no one ever asks about how we were affected personally. How difficult a 10-year-old me, raised in Kuwait for the first 10 years, found adjusting to life in India. How the tin roof of the room on the terrace made sounds of every tree branch, bird, and rain, scaring me. Wearing clothes that did not feel mine, food I did not enjoy, the judgmental tone of those around us on my preferences.

How people changed, presuming that since we did not own stuff, we didn't have anything to our name. How I missed my dad for the months he took reaching us via Jordan by car/ship. How I did not understand the education system in India for a few months.

It was much more than just the war.

When you are a child belonging neither here, nor there, not having had enough time to process either nationality, you are left feeling misplaced. My sense of identity got reshaped. Broken and consequently, restructured.

Before the war, I was just a girl who lived in Kuwait. My brain never needed to process who I am or where I belong but when you must leave your home and move to a different country, the world questions who you are.

When the war came, it swept away big parts of my innocence, in more ways than one. It brought forth the reality of the people around me. The feeling of being adrift in a sea of people will stay with me forever.

During the war, a couple of weeks later, we were living with five families in an apartment. Different foods, different ways of life. All under one roof. Yet, it wasn't very odd for a ten-year-old because everyone was known to me. They were all just 'Uncles and Aunts'.

Once I came to India though, I started learning that 'Uncles and Aunts' are people not related to you. People related to you are all defined by a specific name. Chachi, Chacha, Tau, Phupha etc. That everyone expects you to be a certain way if you belong to a community.

You are almost expected to cater to the stereotype predefined.

My first "*Where are you from?*" on the school bus in India, displaced my sense of self completely. "*Indian*" I responded. But that was not enough. With parents from different states in India, and mannerisms not like them, the questionee ground into knowing where I had come from. Thereon, I felt the need to explain in detail to everyone who asked me, "Born and raised in Kuwait, my mom is from Maharashtra, Amravati and my dad is from Madhya Pradesh, Gwalior. No, it's not a love marriage. My grandfather saw my mom at a wedding and asked for her hand in marriage to his son."

You can see a lot of what the Indian mindset is like, in that description of my origin.

The question "*Where are you from?*" has been a thorn in my side since then. I ramble into the details of my life, afraid of being boxed and still trying to fit into a community. Always ticked off by the need of people to ask that question to find a way to relate with me. My insane need to connect with everyone in some way in all those years, led me to unravel my origin and life lived in as much detail as I could go into.

Now that I think of it, I may have almost sounded crazy to the few who just asked the question with no other thing in mind to talk about.

Throughout my whole life, I was too Kuwaiti for India, too Indian for Kuwait!

After the war, life in Kuwait also changed drastically. The 'us vs them' mentality grew and Western culture seeped in. People got more wary of wasting time and money on socializing. The walls around every family grew, letting in only the few who could connect deeply.

It was very unnerving and yet, empowering for a child growing into the teens to realize that I am much more than just 'Indian.' Though, it took a recent comment about *"How would you know about India? You have never lived there."* for me to realize that I am a global citizen and not just one nationality.

As I mention in my award winning book **Strong Roots Have No Fear**, it is only by the grace of my strong value system that I was able to recover my "being".

I was and will be, way more than is expected of me at face value. Something I taught to my kids early.

You are 100% Indian and 100% American

The children of the world today are not just 'part this part that' because the world is expanding daily and the borders of culture, religion and self-identity are often shifting.

You Have to Respect Every Country You Belong To

I never had a Kuwaiti passport, in spite of being born and spending the majority of my life there. I am not Indian by mindset. I now live my life in America and am an American citizen but am Indian in a lot of my ways, probably my accent too. I love Kuwait for my childhood memories. I love India for my culture and values. I love America for the life I have today. Each one deserves my respect and that of my children.

No Matter Where You Are, Family is Home

We left Kuwait with nothing. We were okay! I came to the USA with a bag of stuff. I was okay! As long as you have loved ones around you, you will always be okay. Your family values define you, not your surroundings or the things you own.

Your Identity Defines You

People will always try to shake up your confidence - to box you; to color you in the shades they prefer. Who you are, is much more than what people believe. No matter what you are called, know that what defines you, are your actions and words. A huge reason for me writing my Sparkling Me, children's books series.

Divisiveness Leads to Fractures in People

This may seem like a no brainer, but it needs to be said. We need to start one at a time, to stop creating borders around our identity. When countries go to war, you have to be by the side of what is right. At a cost to yourself! But above all, you must stand for inclusion and be empathetic to the struggles of all involved.

"My identity might begin with the fact of my race, but it didn't, couldn't end there. At least, that is what I choose to believe." - *Barack Obama*

Make your belief system so strong that no amount of displacement can shatter your being. Find faith and hope within and share it, like the spark in the darkness we all live in.

ABOUT ADITI WARDHAN SINGH

Multi award winning author and self-publishing coach, Aditi is an authoritative voice on cultural sensitivity and self-empowerment. She founded RaisingWorldChildren.com, an online and print publication for multicultural families and authored the parenting book Strong Roots Have No Fear. From a childhood of feeling like the Girl from Nowhere, she grew to believing that we belong everywhere. Her books How Our Skin Sparkles, Sparkles of Joy, Small or Tall - We Sparkle After All teach kids about acceptance - of self and others.

In her spare time, a trained Indian classical dancer in Kathak & Bharatnatyam, Aditi likes to choreograph dance recitals to be performed at local festivals & have impromptu dance parties with her children.

Website: https://raisingworldchildren.com/

Instagram: https://www.instagram.com/raisingworldchildren/

Section II
Difficult Conversations

Chapter 10

Talking to Children about Racial Equality
Ronda Bowen

We stood in the driveway, my then five-year-old watching the movers load our entire house onto their truck. The summer sun beat down hard, and I scurried around making sure that the two men had enough hydration while they did their work.

"Momma, why does that man have dark brown skin?", my son asked. It was a question I had not anticipated, but perhaps I should have. We were moving from a college town in Northern California to a much smaller college town in Illinois, to attend graduate school at Northern Illinois University. One of our little city's qualities was that it didn't have a whole lot of diversity. I was aware of that fact – but I was not aware of how being in such a homogenous population could affect my son's perception of the world.

"Because he has more of a substance called melanin in his skin than we do in ours", was my response. It satisfied the scientist in him, and I left things at that for the time being. It did make me realize that even though he had been around diverse people, we hadn't discussed it. Turns out that avoiding race as a topic was a mistake - and not for some of the problems (we will get into later) that can crop up when parents avoid the topic of racial equality with kids - but because I had not really prepared him for witnessing racism. Over the course of the two years following the moving day,

we wound up having many conversations about race and racial equality.

We Cannot Afford to Be *Colorblind*

For a while, there was an inkling of a thought that if you were raising your child, you were raising your child to 'not see color'. While the intent behind this was to erase barriers between children, it had an unfortunate side effect. In 2016, Marie-Anne Suizzo presented her research in *The Washington Post* on what happens when we teach children that skin color should be ignored. In her article, *'The Danger of Teaching Children to Be 'Colorblind'*, she wrote:

"But white anxiety starts during childhood, when white children are often taught that all skin colors are equal and should therefore be ignored. This is called "colorblind socialization" and many white parents practice it with their children early on, in a well-intentioned but highly damaging attempt to prevent racism. The way colorblind socialization plays out is to avoid any conversations about skin color. If a child brings it up, you must quickly correct and silence them and explain that mentioning someone's skin color is rude, and racist.

"The problem with this strategy is that instead of nurturing children's natural curiosity about differences, it teaches them to be wary and to feel ashamed if they even notice their friends' skin color."

In the example where my son had asked me about the man's skin color, if I had hushed him quickly, instead of responding to his question, I might have taught him that it's not okay to notice skin color – or worse, that skin color and tone is something to be ashamed of.

Race and Racial Identity Are Things We Notice

We cannot just ignore a person's race. Not only because many cultural differences are at play, but also because unfortunately, people do treat others differently based on the color and tone of their skin. When we moved to rural Illinois, this is something that slapped us in the face – quite rudely, in fact.

I grew up in the San Francisco Bay Area, where even though my schools were not as diverse as some of the schools in the area, racial diversity was prominent. Despite the prevalence of individuals with a variety of racial backgrounds, I had also noticed that teachers treated black students differently from white students. **In the 1990s, Hip Hop and R&B artists like Salt & Pepa, Will Smith, and Bel Biv Devoe posters were taped to the walls of my childhood bedroom, while Rodney King, police brutality, the LA Riots, and NWA were on the evening news.** My grandparents used racist terms and hate speech, but that was them, I thought. Surely people still didn't do that.

When I started my master's degree program, I realized how incredibly naive I was about my assumption. I used to think only the elderly and people who live away from civilization, feel that way about people from different cultures. I was constantly shocked at the number of intelligent people displaying extreme levels of ignorance and prejudice.

So, when the episode with my son happened, I knew it was time we discussed racial equality.

Kids Understand More Than We Think They Do

Talking about inequality is rough. We need to prepare children for the injustices they might face or witness in the world – as tough as that fact is to stomach. So, I sat down, and began a discussion that was far more difficult for me than it was for my kid.

"Sometimes," I said, *"people treat others differently…and even badly…just because of the color of that person's skin."*

"That's stupid."

"Yes, it is, but it doesn't change the fact that it happens. You might have a friend at school like I did, who maybe is being treated differently than others because of how they look."

62

"That's wrong. People shouldn't do that." And that's the gist of our conversation. But I didn't stop there. I told my son about hate speech and words and their effect. And we kept having open discussions about race, and about how sometimes people of color, don't get a fair break in life because others believe falsely that they don't deserve to have certain things.

Helping Children Stand Up Against Racial Bias

A year after all those talks, the principal called me because they had my son in their office. He had gotten into a fight as a first grader with a second grader. When I asked him what happened, he said that the second grader had used the N-word to refer to one of my son's first-grade friends. My son yelled, *"That's hate speech!"* and pushed the other child.

I was furious that my son was being punished but not the other child involved. I explained that yes, it was wrong to push someone and that we would discuss it along with the school's punishment. But the other child had made my son feel that his friend was being threatened. And what my son did, despite going about it the wrong way, was a positive thing in acknowledging that the words used were NOT okay and he was right in standing up for his friend.

Several years later, he again showed courage against racial injustice, when a teacher at his middle school displayed extreme bias in the way that he taught the non-white children in his class. My son explained to me that he was upset by this and wanted to stand up. I encouraged him to report the incidents he had witnessed. That teacher was let go.

We must stand by children, who take the initiative in fighting racism. One of the reasons it is so important to discuss race and racial injustice, is that kids don't ignore injustice when they see it. If we want to move past this era of racism, we need kids to grow up knowing that it's NOT okay to ignore it.

In the words of Martin Luther King Jr., *"Freedom is never voluntarily given by the oppressor; it must be demanded by the oppressed."* Let us teach our children how to stand up for the oppressed by refusing to let them be "colorblind."

ABOUT RONDA BOWEN

Ronda Bowen wears a lot of hats. Ronda runs her own editorial consulting business, a specialty boutique, and three blogs. She leads an active multi-level Girl Scout troop, serves as Fundraising Director for the charity JB Dondolo (just honored by the Dallas chapter of the UN for their work on SDG 6 – Clean Water). She also works with a local branch of the Juvenile Arthritis Foundation to organize their annual Jingle Bell Run. She has a master's degree in philosophy, and publishes articles on social and political philosophy, ethics, what we can learn about ourselves from pop culture, and environmentalism. She has served as Senior Editor for Equanimity Magazine since its inception in 2009, and she is working on launching SNARK! a magazine dedicated to literary fiction, poetry, and snarky social commentary. Ms. Bowen loves archery, hiking, and kayaking, and being unplugged as much as possible.

Website: http://rondabowen.com

Instagram: https://instagram.com/justasecular

Chapter 11

Finding Cultural Context in a Global Setting
Devishobha Chandramouli

"Choose your self-presentations carefully, for what starts out as a mask may become your face."
— Erving Goffman.

"Where are you from?" asked the store-guy at a small mom-and-pop store. We were the quintessential immigrant student group, hungry to lap up every chance we got to explore our host country. We were freshly suffused with the early dawn magnificence of the Grand Canyon, and it seemed somehow appropriate when my friend answered, *"From Phoenix, Arizona."* *After all, we were a student group from Arizona State University, Phoenix, visiting Grand Canyon on a winter break.*

As we were leaving the store, another friend of mine piped in, *"You know, I would have responded with 'India' for that question."*

Inadvertently, this guy plunged me into revisiting the meaning of home in a globalized world.

Much later, I realized that the simple question, *"Where are you from?"* is a particular source of agony for many Third Culture Kids (TCK). Coined by the American sociologist <u>Ruth Hill Useem</u>, the term 'Third Culture Kid' refers to a child who has spent a significant part of their formative years outside their parents' culture. Not surprisingly, those growing up in a different culture tend to attach themselves and merge with their adopted culture, along with their birth culture, creating a unique culture of their own: a third culture.

The simple question can trigger an identity crisis - do they mean my country of birth? Or my current nationality? The place I was born or where my parents live?

Third Culture Kids are often seen omitting parts of their story or explaining themselves unduly to make their story more palatable for the listener. Surprisingly(not!) enough, the conversation can lead further into, *"No, but where are you really from?"*

I come from a country that is the true essence of a melting point of cultures - 29 States; All with their unique languages; hundreds of cuisines; unique clothes and weaves; color; accents, lifestyles. India has so many unique cultures that you could be 200 km from your birthplace and still be experiencing a completely different culture. No cultural practice surprises Indians because there are so many layers of them embedded in every culture - each of them is unique, flavorful, and has a lot of history behind them.

As a child, I was hardly aware that I was only naturally experiencing what was set to become the gold standard for globalization - an integration of cultures.

A 2015 U.S Bureau of Labor Statistics study suggests the average worker today held ten different jobs before they touched 40, with these numbers only set to go upward in the future. Today's kids are growing up in a world where they will only live in more places and explore diverse careers than ever before, and experience changes in an unprecedented manner.

So what identity anchors can they hope to tether themselves to?

As sociologist Ruth Van Reken states, *"The third culture kid builds relationships to all the cultures, while not having full ownership in any. Although elements from each are assimilated into the third culture kid's life experience, the sense of belonging is in relationship to others of the same background, other Third Culture Kids."*

TCKs are most comfortable around other people who have experienced the transience and diversity similar to their own. What draws them to each other is a sense of curiosity and a restless vulnerability that leads them to develop a sensitivity to multiple cultures - including their own!

This famous quote from Janet Kagan says it all, *"You'll surprise you more than they will."*

This sense of curiosity mingled with vulnerability presents the perfect ground for more in-depth explorations around identity and belonging, laying the foundation for the seminal question around culture:

"What are the cultural roots that are important to you, and why?"

One of those questions that seek deeper reassurances than just answers, demanding more show than tell!

Here are a bunch of cultural reintegration strategies useful to nurture a strong sense of identity while also fostering an openness toward other cultures.

Integrate culture through celebrations

Every cultural practice is birthed and bred in history, some of which are literally thousands of years old. What's known to us today as tradition and cultural practice is something that started a few hundred or even a few thousand years ago - as a creative adaptation to a life situation through adjustments in food and clothing, which subsequently leads to a change in mood, energy, and community living. Festivals, the precursors of celebrations, are the perfect opportunities to start conversations around culture. Thus, leading to a deeper understanding of their own people and history.

A brilliant example would be a festival called *Ram Navami* that is celebrated just before the onset of summer among Indians. The festival brings people together to worship a prominent deity called Rama, following which a sweet liquid and soaked lentils are distributed to the crowd gathered. This food served and distributed, popularly known as *Prasad'* in Indian culture, is, in reality, preparation for the upcoming scorching summer. The sweet liquid is made of natural organic spices and ingredients that reduce the body's temperature. The lentils mixed with lemon and coconut boost digestive hygiene, anticipating the scorching months ahead.

Conversations that dig more in-depth and explore the significance of cultural practices have the potential not just to connect our kids to their root cultures but lay the groundwork for independent exploration of the connection between man and everything around them - through the past, present and future.

Leverage Stories

Just like festivals and celebrations, many cultures express themselves beautifully through stories. Indeed, there can be no better tool than storytelling to reinforce *Social and Emotional Learning*, a topic that frequently shows up in discussions around school curricula that promote mental agility. Storytelling intricately weaves narratives between feelings, emotions, expressions, thoughts, and actions of people who lived before us. Stories provide a fertile ground for the listener's imagination while creating a deep understanding of the connection between thoughts and actions - and, subsequently, consequences. What better way to enrich their understanding of cultures - replete with the whys and hows? Storytelling also inculcates deep respect for the process of evolution of a 'culture'. The same strategy can be adopted before or after every visit to a historical place, regardless of relevance to your own culture.

Use Natural Opportunities

Language is a powerful connection to culture, simply because languages evolve in tandem with a culture, carrying all the markings of other influences on them. A language spoken in a culture influenced by another will always allow for the infusion of new words into the existing language, and carry them through time, long after the influence has faded in other aspects of people's lives. Hence, it is essential to speak in your native language at home. Create opportunities for them to learn the written script of the language. The depth of a language and a deeper understanding of culture lie in the recesses of literature.

Use Resources to Drive Conversations

Many excellent books, both fiction and non-fiction, themed around multi-generational families finding their moorings in different cultures. But if I have to quote one book that opened my eyes to whole new perspectives on cultural expectations, it is 'Everything You Never Told Me' By Celeste Ng. The book portrays the life of an immigrant family. The parents transfer their expectations on culture-difference management to their children based on their own experiences while settling into a new culture, only to find out later that their kids were facing a whole different set of challenges to tragic consequences.

An excellent place to reconcile differences in cultural understanding is to begin by asking your child about the cultural differences they encounter. Use seminal resources on cultural understanding like 'Van Reken and Pollock's seminal book Third Culture Kids: The Experience of Growing Up Among Worlds' to begin discussions around cultural confusion.

We can only resolve struggles around identity by consistently being open to discussions and conversations around the topic and ensuring you always provide a haven for transitions.

See culture through their eyes.

As parents, our natural expectation is for our children to understand our culture. But it is essential to see their world through their cultural lens. Not doing so might look like a one-way thrust upon them to conform, while they struggle with both sides' expectations. An excellent start to understanding their world is - through their friends. Create opportunities to mingle as a family with their friends and families of similar cultures and other diverse cultures.

ABOUT DEVISHOBHA CHANDRAMOULI

Devishobha Chandramouli is the founder of Kidskintha - a Global Conscious Parenting And Education Collective that has evolved into an authentic resource platform for parents and educators online with global perspectives on education, emotional intelligence, child psychology, and behavioral development and a recipient of the BusinessWorld 40 Under 40 Achievers' Award. She is also Vice-President of Early Childhood Association, India and a facilitator for the UNESCO Futures of Education initiative in India. Devishobha has also lent her voice to some major international publications like the Huffington Post, Entrepreneur Media, Addicted2Success, LifeHack, Tiny Buddha, and many more. Her other loves include cooking, singing, and being goofy around the house.

Website: www.kidskintha.com

Instagram: https://instagram.com/kidskintha

Chapter 12

Pondering Over Privilege
Lucretia Marie Anderson

*"Being able to live without having to be defined
by your skin color is the hallmark of privilege."*
– Luvvie Ajayi.

H ow do we have conversations with our children about privilege, when there are so many types to consider?

I identify as African American, a single mother of two children, an educator, and an artist. I have insisted on doing what is necessary to give my children what I perceive to be the advantages of a private education. But I feel that it comes at a bit of a cost as far as navigating the in and out of privilege in America in particular. My kids have benefitted from this educational privilege, but they have also been hurt in this setting by their lack of privileges based on their skin color and socio-economic status.

They feel the pinch of not being able to see, do, and have many of the things that their more affluent peers may have. They have also had to endure comments and misunderstandings about their character based on misconceptions and stereotypes of people of color. Yet, at the same time, they have so many other privileges as able-bodied, well-educated citizens of the United States. My focus has been to help them understand and acknowledge what privilege is for good and bad, to cultivate their own happiness, confidence, and a global mindset.

The first step in the conversation about privilege starts with the understanding that it comes in different degrees and types. If you are reading this, chances are you already have had many forms of privilege. In my experience, it doesn't help to know that, unless you know what to do with it.

For seven years, I taught at a private middle school for girls. The school where I taught in Richmond, Virginia is predominantly white, and for the majority of my time there I was the only faculty member of color at our school. I have seen first-hand how an inability for children to see or acknowledge their own privilege, not only hurts the underprivileged but themselves as well. Privileged children can become deeply unhappy and dissatisfied, when they aren't guided to think outside of themselves; or dont have adults modeling this behavior for them. This, of course, can manifest in a number of behavioral and social problems.

Growing up, I was always admonished for not finishing my food or appreciating something I was given by being told to think of the poor children in any number of developing countries. This form of guilt-tripping a child into gratitude would likely be frowned upon now, and it didn't necessarily work then, but it has its roots in something worth examining - and that is gratitude.

In the 7th grade at my former school, I co-taught a character development class that focused on several issues and topics surrounding identity formation. During our unit on diversity and inclusion, we spent some time discussing privilege before introducing some concepts of social justice concepts. It was important for our students to delve deeply (well, as much as they can at that stage of development) in understanding the privileges that they have largely, coming from a majority white-centric culture and predominantly middle to upper middle-class social status. We were careful to help our students understand why and how they have the privileges that they do and the difference between using their privilege to support justice versus charity.

While it is hard sometimes to see where and when these lessons will sprout, the seeds have been planted not only to foster gratitude but to help them understand the responsibilities of privilege as a global citizen.

With my own children, I began in their early years, as young as 5 or 6 years old, to help them navigate and understand what it means to have brown skin; be afforded many of the privileges of their more affluent peers – beach vacations, first-class education, tons of culture, consistent meals and a comfortable home; and yet still not have the privilege of being a paler color of skin in a culture where that is celebrated.

This is what I wanted my children to know. I believe it would benefit all children to know these things, especially those who are being reared to be globally minded citizens:

- If you live in Western culture, if you have any level of education beyond grade school, if you have access to books and technology, if you have typically developing physical or mental abilities - you have privilege! This does not mean that some things aren't difficult for you and that you face no adversity or discrimination, but you still have advantages that can lead to having more opportunities in life than others may. Acknowledging this will not take away your privilege, but it does allow the conditions of others to be seen and recognized.

- Many people are granted privileges for no more than what family, ethnicity, skin color, ability, hetero-normative, or socio-economic class that they were born with. This certainly doesn't make them better or less worthy of human rights and dignity than anyone else.

- In America and of course, much of Western Culture, white privilege prevails. If you choose to learn more about white privilege, an incredibly useful resource to define and explain the concept is *teachingtolerance.org*. I found this information there:

  > *Author Francis E. Kendall defines white privilege as "having greater access to power and resources than people of color [in the same situation] do."*

  > Teaching Tolerance also explains that what it means is, *"White people become more likely to move through the world with an expectation that their needs be readily met. People of color move through the world knowing their needs are on the margins. Recognizing this means recognizing where gaps exist."*

- When you are granted a privilege, it is your responsibility not only to be in gratitude for that privilege, but to use it for good whenever possible. I believe this is especially true if your privilege is based on a trait or status you inherited but didn't earn. If you have the opportunity to help someone, who does not share the same privilege that you have, do so for the sake of human goodness. It takes nothing away from you to do that.

Here are a few great ways to start these conversations at a young age:

Find Age-Appropriate Books about Different Forms of Privilege

Reading picture books with your children that feature stories of privilege. A quick Google search can help you find any number of books on a variety of topics around privilege. Raising Luminaries, a website devoted to "Igniting the Kind and Brilliant Leaders of Tomorrow" has a list called *Captivating Kids Stories* to recognize privilege. Helping kids understand all different kinds of privilege in digestible stories can go a long way.

Use Teachable Moments to Build Gratitude

Leaning into examples from your own life as they arise. Are you able to stay at home with your children and take them on meaningful explorations of their community? Do you have friends that are differently abled? Pointing out why and how can do certain things while others can't, can be a powerful tool to help understand privilege.

Try Gifting to Build Community

Teach alternatives to luxury and receiving, while demonstrating how community gifting, donation, and upcycling help to strengthen your community and meet others.

Go Outside of Your Immediate Neighborhood

Taking a trip to another part of town to experience what others in another part of your community experience can help give a good deal of perspective.

Starting a conversation as early as makes sense for your kids, about what privilege is and having gratitude for their own is the spark of happiness, pride, confidence, and empathy. **It is important not to view privilege as a lens through which one is put to shame, but rather to educate and empower.**

My hope is that having a good understanding of privilege will help us all to have a more open dialogue and empathetic global communities.

ABOUT LUCRETIA MARIE ANDERSON

Lucretia Marie Anderson is a mother of two, writer, educator, life coach and theatre artist, who currently resides in Richmond, Virginia. She is a former arts and cultural education administrator for the Smithsonian Institution's Discovery Theatre and the Folger Shakespeare Library in Washington, DC. She has been a middle school teacher of English and Theatre and has written for *Richmond Mom's Blog* and a compendium on Arts Integration for Intellect Books.

Lucretia is the founder of Joyful Muse Coaching, a service dedicated to transformational life coaching, mindfulness training, and parenting coaching. She has written performance pieces for *If You Could See Me*, a project dedicated to raising awareness and advocacy around mental health issues, and is an advocate for adolescent mental wellness and LGBTQ youth. She spends most of the time reading, performing, or taking the family on various adventures.

Website: www.joyfulmusecoaching.com

Instagram: Instagram.com/lucretianspires

Chapter 13

Skin Color
Sybil Jones

I am a black woman, married to a black man, raising black children in America in 2020.

Is it scary at times? YES!

As a nation, we've made improvements, but there are still so many things happening in this world to our black and brown people.

We see things happening on the news every day. Sometimes we may want to ignore it or pretend it is not happening to our children or us and continue living in our bubble. But the truth is, it is happening to you!

The issues we see happening to others because of skin color is everyone's problem.

Just because people choose NOT to have a conversation about the many issues surrounding skin color, does not mean it doesn't exist or that it will go away. It is an uncomfortable but necessary conversation.

Now, do not dismiss what I am about to say from this point forward. To help you understand my world and how others can help raise global children and hopefully change mindsets (their own and others), I am going to share a brief glimpse of my life.

I wake up every morning, look in the mirror, and see an educated, strong, wonderful wife, mother, and a beautiful black woman. I see my educated, hard-working, dedicated, handsome black husband and father of our children in front of me. I also see three intelligent, beautiful, strong-willed, independent black children, who are set out to change the world. These are all the things I see and want the world to see.

But I know that everyone does not see that. Some see BLACK people; and some have a misconception of the color of our skin as being black equals bad. It equals uneducated. The color of our skin makes many uncomfortable and fearful.

T.V. has portrayed black men as thugs for years. Black women are portrayed as single mothers with too many children to care for, without receiving some form of government assistance. Black children are portrayed as loud and ignorant.

Before my family walks out of the door each morning, I tell them that I love them and to have a great day. I actually tell my children to **"Mind Their Business and Mind Their Goals. To always remember to Know You Be You Love You®."** So far, my morning is much like every other human being. But then it suddenly changes once each member of my family takes their last step off of our porch to enter the harsh reality of the world. The reality that they may be judged purely by the color of their skin.

"I look to a day when people will not be judged by the color of their skin, but by the content of their character." - Martin Luther King, Jr.

Often, I catch myself thinking, *"Oh, I pray no one profiles my husband. He has a hoodie on and a backpack walking to catch the train this morning because it's cool out."* I mean, he iss dressed like everyone else heading to the train, who isn't wearing their suit or military uniform. But he is black! And for some, the color of his skin in that hoodie makes people nervous.

Have you had to worry about something just because you have darker skin than those around you? If not, do know, it is real! It is a concern for so many mothers, wives, children, and other family members, when their loved ones walk out of the door.

Being a mother of black girls, we have regular discussions about how they may be perceived differently than their peers. School and hanging out with friends is what you do as a tween and teen. However, I must tell my children to be mindful of how loud they may laugh or joke because they may be considered hoodlums or out to cause trouble. When all they are doing is being a teenager like all the other kids around them. But the color of their skin erases all childlike activities.

As I continue to work on my Ph.D. from The University of Life, I take note of others' reactions when it comes to discussing issues in America, when it has to do with black and brown skin.

I watch how others turn away from communities that have a large population of black and brown families. I pay attention to school ratings, when the majority of students are black and brown; the test scores being very close, yet the ratings are a 3 versus 10.

Have you ever been told that someone refuses to send a child to a school because they do not want their child to be uncomfortable? Uncomfortable because the majority do not look like them.

Yes, I had to catch myself. I had to stop in my tracks before I spoke. I bit my tongue and put on a smile. I made the decision to listen, not just hear, but listen because it was clear that the individual did not have an open mind. Or maybe, when living in one's own bubble, people truly miss out on what's going on in the real world.

How can you ensure your family isn't missing out on what's going on in the real world, and how can you ensure Global Children are being raised?

Open Your Eyes

See others for who they are, not just by the color of their skin. It's ok to see skin color. We all see it. Let's stop the misconceptions and get to know one another for the individual person.

Have Real Conversations

All lessons begin at home. Teach children what you want them to know. Love and acceptance of others. We may all look different on the outside, but we all have the same organs keeping us alive on the inside.

Be an Example

Diversify your circle. If everyone looks like you, step out and build relationships with those who do not.

Is it my responsibility as a black woman to educate every single person, who does not look like me? The answer is NO! But I do feel it is my responsibility to share my story, experiences, and live my life to the fullest. Hopefully, my stories will help others remove their blinders.

When I walk out of my home, I walk out as Sybil. I present to you, Sybil Jones. A black woman who is proud to be who she is and loves who she is! A woman who loves people and loves to surround herself with **ALL** people. And if people refuse to accept me for me or want to dismiss and mistreat me because of the color of my skin, it is their loss, not mine!

I see the color of everyone's skin, but it does not matter to me. Stop saying that you do not see color. See color, notice your privilege, see the injustice and work to change it.

Let us take off our blinders, move out of our bubbles, and work to be a better world.

ABOUT SYBIL JONES

Sybil is a Navy wife of 18 years, mother of three (tween and teen girls), and owner of a silly little Maltese named Carlos. She's a graduate of The University of Memphis, where she received her B.B.A. in Logistics and Marketing. She's currently working on her Ph.D. from The University of Life. Her passion is to empower others in life with her message of Know You Be You Love You®. She enjoys sharing her experiences and advice about life to empower others. You can find her having fun on her site, Mamas and Coffee®. Her writing style is simple and airy. She is also the owner of Sybil Talks. A platform promoting self-love and body image from the skinny perspective. She is also the host of Milspouse Conversations™, an online space, and virtual monthly meetups for military spouses to have real, raw and supportive conversations about military spouse life.

Website: www.mamasandcoffee.com

Facebook: www.facebook.com/momjonz

Chapter 14

Discrimination
Shalini Tyagi

"Injustice anywhere is a threat to justice everywhere."
- Martin Luther King, Jr.

Our future generations are going to inherit a world that might be divided on many fronts, but it will be a multicultural world all the same. The adults of tomorrow will be global people in a much truer sense.

So, who is a global person? And what is a multicultural world? Is it a world of coexistence across races and national extraction?

As always everything progressive is accompanied by some challenges. There is so much being said in terms of accepting and adapting to a global lifestyle.

Yet, what is the one thing that is still a stumbling block in this approach? It is Mindset, not physical borders.

The mindset of stereotypes and subtle judgments, which leads to subconscious discrimination. This is what creates an imbalance.

When you register the word 'discrimination', you might picture people being abused, shouted upon or segregated on many levels.

I will begin by explaining why I say you do not "hear" the word discrimination, when you **register** it. This is because the word 'discrimination' is just not heard, but quickly processed and you visualize the above scenarios. There are chances that after understanding the full impact of the word, you deny its very existence.

Someone asked me *"Are you saying there is discrimination amongst us?"* Despite this issue staring in the face most of the time, we fail to recognize it, let alone deal with it.

Let's introspect...

Is every part of the globe treating everyone equally? Does every person get the same respect despite their race, gender, physical appearance, financial standing or place of origin?

Can you answer both the above questions in the affirmative to the best of your knowledge?

If even in the slightest doubt, then things need to be worked upon at the basic level.

The basic level needs the phasing out of this obstacle, so that we are one step closer to a global mindset. **My idea of phasing out discrimination from the upbringing of kids is through equality in treatment.**

What is Discrimination?

The unjust or prejudicial treatment of different categories of people, especially on the grounds of race, age or sex is discrimination.

On a cold winter night of 1893, Mahatma Gandhi was thrown off a train in South Africa. He was asked to leave a first class "whites only" compartment as he was a man of color. When he questioned this bias, he was not only forcibly removed from the compartment but also thrown off the train.

This is discrimination!

When a person assumes or establishes themselves as being better than someone else in anyway, the seeds of discrimination are sown.

Many of us would not agree on this being an issue in the present time, when I quote an incident that is more than a century old. After all, no one is getting thrown off trains for their skin color anymore.

I agree, it is not present in an "in your face" way most of the time, but the subtle undercurrent can be felt lingering.

Let me draw your attention to an article recently published by CNBC and I quote the heading:

"It will take 100 years for women to earn the same as men at this rate."

In simpler terms: a woman is paid 80 cents to every $1 her male counterpart earns. That is for the same work done and in the year 2019. Let this sink in! And this is happening more than 120 years later, when Gandhi was thrown off a train.

If this is not discrimination than what is?

These are just a few examples to support the argument that it is still more rampant than we are ready to accept.

There is no right time to start doing what is right. Anytime you do the right thing, is the right time!

We Indians have always been prejudiced against the female gender and their physical appearance; with a special emphasis on skin color.

Being a woman, you are stereotyped and not expected to break the mold. Personally, I can vouch for the number of times a woman is required to prove her mettle in every arena. Anything that belittles someone is still discrimination, even if it is widely accepted.

How do you start doing right?

Identify the Problem and Act

Sensitize our kids to predicaments that pave way to any form of discrimination.

Small instances like when someone on the subway decides not to sit next to another person, due to their physical appearance or the way they are dressed. Or looking at a person differently because of a disability.

Check these subtle hints that we might be involuntarily giving out. When we do wrong, we must accept it and explain to our children why they need to act better.

Complicated topics like race and religion are what baffle kids the most.

In grade 5, my son joined a new school. On the first day, I went to drop him to class and the moment he introduced himself, one of the boys commented on his religion. I was stumped for a few seconds, but then I smiled and asked the child whether it mattered? To which he simply nodded a NO.

Kids are just kids, curious and at times confused. What we can do is hold their hand and guide them through this labyrinth with our understanding. We must work towards making them recognize that no particular person is better or worse. We are different - but with equal rights.

Having mutual respect towards their peers gives children the understanding to have respect for each other's beliefs and practices.

Kids can learn how to be respectful around another's faith, while being grounded on their own. The possibility of discrimination towards any faith is nipped in the bud.

Boys and girls who receive equal treatment at home can understand, when they see discrimination based on gender and confront it. Equal opportunities based on an individual's ability, not if they are a particular gender.

Changes in behavior towards people because of their financial standing, makes it a norm for our kids to discriminate based on money. An affluent neighbor might be a good individual to command our respect, but that does not diminish the level of regard for the not-so-rich neighbor as a person.

We are addressing kids here, so I would not delve into highly sensitive topics that might not be of much relevance to kids at this age. One thing that is of paramount value is what we teach them young, as it goes a long way.

For those of us who are global people and travel much, even a minor incident stops us in our tracks and compels us to think. **It takes a lot of courage to apprehend the wrong and stand for what is right. Especially, if it does not affect us directly.**

Martin Luther King aptly said, *"Any injustice anywhere threatens justice everywhere"*, as any wrong that goes unchecked acts as an example. It paves the way for others to commit the same offence.

Every slight that we might let pass, are the ones that need to be curbed for a tolerant multicultural future; for a global society to be free of any barriers of inequality and unfairness.

A better world that can borrow a few lines from one of India's greatest - *"Where the mind is without fear and the head is held high."*

ABOUT SHALINI TYAGI

Shalini is an Indian currently living in the UAE. She is mother to two school going kids - a tween and an eight-year-old. Being an avid reader, writing was just the next natural step.

Shalini tries to keep her writing simple and close to life experiences. A rebel at heart she believes change can be brought for the good, only if one does not stop trying.

Deciding to be a stay-at-home mom after her son was born, she advocates a balanced approach to parenting, where the new can be incorporated with the old.

Website: http://tyagishalinid.com/

Instagram: https://www.instagram.com/tyagideesha/

Chapter 15

Self-Doubt of Cultural Confusion
Sneha Jhanb

*"Culture is the name for what people are
interested in, their thoughts, their models,
the books they read and the speeches they hear."*
- Walter Lippmann

Personally, I have never really fit in a box of anything. A lot of events have made me feel like I did not belong in communities, circles, places, etc.

Over the years though, I have also realized that belonging and fitting in are two different things. Belonging means feeling the love and togetherness, despite who other people are, what their culture is or what their values are. Belonging creates mutual respect.

Fitting in means enforcing values of another, to feel the love and togetherness. Fitting in creates confusion. Fitting in creates the wrongness of being different.

When it comes to cultural diversity and living in a global world and on top of that being a parent, I believe understanding the difference between belonging and fitting in, helps a lot.

Our Life in Vegas

We moved to Vegas in 2010. Never in my life had I thought we would move to a place that is nicknamed "Sin City." Both my kids were born in the suburbs of Vegas (Henderson).

When I became a mom, I did not have many Indian friends (that is my origin). I joined a meetup group that had a wide diversity in terms of culture. We had Indian, British, African Americans, local Nevadians or Las Vegans, Armenian, Dutch, German, Christians, Hindu, Atheists, Mormons in this group. We had our kids around the same time; and most of us subsequently had a second kid around the same time as well.

Many of them were excited to learn more about *Holi*. We used to play this festival of color in the park. I was interested to learn about how they celebrated Christmas at their home and the importance of the Christmas tree.

But more than learning from each other's religion, the one thing I really learned from this group was being there for each other at difficult times. When someone delivered, we signed up for meal trains and sent food to the new mommy's house for 2-3 weeks straight. We volunteered together; and one of them encouraged the kids to participate in volunteering and led kid-related volunteering activities.

Each one of us had a different cultural background. We all had an amazing local support system. I learned a lot about upbringing of kids, discipline, etc. through this group. Some believed in vaccines and some did not. Some were atheists and some were religious. It was never an issue to fit in the group or belong. Since everyone was from somewhere else it felt most inclusive.

Moving to Atlanta, Georgia

A few years ago, I moved to a suburb of Atlanta. Here, I am mostly surrounded by the Indian community. I have not seen many communities interact much with each other. I have seen more segregation in the Indian community itself. Each language (based on which state they came from in India) has their own group, cultural get-togethers, and celebrations.

My husband and I belong to two different sub-cultures from India. He is from the North and I am from the Western part of India. We grew up speaking different languages. When it comes to fitting into our own cultures, we are different than most because we have a mini-multi cultural thing going on in our own household.

I must say I have found some friends here, but I have not found a place in the community, where I feel like I belong and can be myself without trying to fit in yet. I do believe it takes time to adjust to a new city especially for adults.

Thankfully, the kids have been making friends more easily at school and have adjusted well.

Cultural Confusion for Kids

What worries me the most after my move here, is which culture do I infuse into my children? They identify themselves as Americans. They identify their parents as Indians. They currently are not mature enough to understand the multiculturalism that lies beyond just being an Indian and an American.

They do not yet understand that some of their new Indian friends speak different languages at home; and that their parents came from a different place in India and have a different influence on them than we have on our kids.

The only similarity they see is Indian parents having American children!

On top of that, my kids are not identified as Americans by their other American friends (white and black) because they do not look like them. They speak like them, they are growing up playing the same games, watching similar shows but their looks matter in that case.

Thankfully, no one has called my kids "Indian" (other than their Indian grandparents), so they are not facing the truth yet at their tender ages.

My Solution to My Confusion

I have decided to move beyond labels and teach my children that culture is not just about where your roots are. Culture is also about where you are being planted and where you plan to bloom. Culture is about adaptation and making it your own in your own beautiful personal way.

I am raising citizens of the world. Giving them an opportunity to learn about so many different cultures at their tender ages is a blessing. I want to switch this self-talk around confusion into a learning opportunity instead, and have the children understand each other's culture and learn from each other.

When I lived in Vegas, I had the Mormon missionaries stop by my house sometimes so that they could share with me their culture. I was getting started on understanding where they came from and who they were. I did not want to convert myself but just understanding others helps us understand and empathize with different cultures better.

Maybe, we could do the same here in Atlanta. We could learn from the Southerners, from the local black and white community, from the Bengalis, from the Tamilians and Telegus, from the Maharastrians, from the Sikhs, from the North Indians, from the

South Indians, from the Germans, from the Koreans, from all cultures we can.

Just because we moved into a core Indian suburb of Atlanta does not mean we fit in and forget our multicultural growth. It means we have more opportunities to connect consciously in the community and understand each other. It means we have more opportunities to share our life with other people and adapt to new possibilities in our own lives.

As a reader of this book, have you ever faced a self-doubt around your culture? If yes, I want to let you know that you are not alone. As adults and parents in the era of multiculturalism, we are uniquely facing this issue that our parents probably did not have to.

I invite you to write down what a rich multi-cultural life means to you and your family. Once you have that picture clear in your mind, you can then intentionally choose experiences for you and your family, to grow in this world with less confusion and more richness.

One more thing I would love to suggest is having a heart-to-heart talk with your children and understand what they identify themselves as; and learn to accept that. Just because they identify themselves as something you have not identified yourself as, does not mean there is a problem. It means they are adapting to their surroundings and finding their own voice.

As a parent, it is our responsibility to hold space for our children as they grow and understand their identity. **We should share our roots with them, along with accepting where they are planting their roots now. It is an era of cross-culture and fusion. As parents we must do what is best for our children's growth.**

ABOUT SNEHA JHANB

Sneha is the founder of Stress Less with Sneha J and owner of Prosperous Financial Services, LLC. Sneha is an Industrial Engineer turned Certified Mindfulness Teacher, Sound Healing Practitioner and Financial Professional. She helps families connect with their financial and emotional wellbeing and helps achieve stress free prosperity. Her upcoming book Stress Free Prosperity provides real life and simple strategies for the same. She is passionate about connecting consciously in this world and wants to share these values with her 2 boys.

Website: https://stresslesswithsnehaj.com

Instagram: Instagram.com/stresslesswithsnehaj

Chapter 16

Moving Countries
Sherrie McCarthy

"We can't be afraid of change. You may feel very secure in the pond that you are in, but if you never venture out of it, you will never know that there is such a thing as an ocean, a sea. Holding onto something that is good for you now, may be the very reason why you don't have something better."
- C. JoyBell

The idea of moving is daunting for most of us. For kids, it can be a terrifying prospect. And yet it does not have to be so!

A move means confronting the unknown, but it also brings the possibility of personal growth and expansion. It is an experience where you are both, out of your comfort zone and intimately aware of yourself. You get reacquainted with your previously held beliefs and truth about yourself and the world.

For kids, this means they get to have flexibility introduced into their lives at a young age. The price may be a little fear; but the reward is the ability to challenge stereotypes and burst out of the pressure, to blend in with those around them.

I love that in my family exposure to different cultures and places have created confident, open, and accepting children.

Too often, we try to protect our kids by denying them information. We think we can shelter our children from the turmoil that comes with being alive. Although, there are times when less is more in terms of information, when it comes to moving, the more information your kids have the better it is.

Get them involved in the planning aspects of the move as well. Far too often, we confuse fear with danger in our lives. And it is that very fear that can create the danger. I think this is where we as parents can fail our kids, when it comes to preparing them for a move.

Do not deny them the possibility of growth. Do not rush to give them a smooth moving experience, where they magically and seamlessly go from one house and possibly country to another. Allow them to learn to rise above the pain.

Because kids are resilient, the idea of a new home will be scary, especially at first. And all kids are different. I can remember as kids we moved three streets over. Not cities, but streets! I can remember feeling nothing but excitement, whereas my younger brother (by 18 months) would throw up every time he saw a new box packed.

In my present family unit, we are in the unique position of changing countries every few months. As we live on a sailboat, our home comes with us. My youngest knows only this life and rolls with it completely. My oldest was four when we moved onboard, and she still takes it hard when she has yet again to say goodbye to newly made friends.

Knowing that she is going to find it hard, we make sure that her roots to the heart of our home are strong. We have a WhatsApp group with families and friends on both sides of the Atlantic Ocean; and we ensure she has weekly contact and sharing, even if she is absorbed in the life of whatever island we are on. We try the same with new friends, and that consistency helps when some of the newer friendships do not last.

Most people are not moving every few months. However, this change gives you the ability to root into who you are, while taking inspiration on who you can become. Kids look to their parents for direction. If you seem panicked or fearful for them, they will too.

I am not a big fan of *"fake it til you make it"*, unless it is about confidence. I am all for it and in this case in particular! That is not to say that you lie to your children about your fears, but rather frame them in the context of *"It is normal and okay to be afraid. Mommy and daddy have some fears too, but we are also really excited about ... "* This works out better for everyone, rather than refusing to speak about the move or turning into a ball of anxiety.

Kids need to feel loved and secure. A move has the potential to disrupt both, as they fear the loss of contact with friends and family and of course, the loss of their home itself. They may be facing a new language and food on top of that. A move does not need to be a negative event in their lives. In fact, it can be one that teaches them how to grow, handle difficult and conflicting emotions and prepare for change.

To help your kids prepare, try the following -

Make a Family Moving Plan

Kids love to feel involved and the more included they are in the move, the more excited they will be about it. Talk openly about the move and what it involves.

Write down the moving date and with your kids work backward and make a list of all the things that need to be done. Create a chart with stickers for when each task is completed. Having the ability to contribute keeps them with a sense of control and pride.

Research your New Home Ahead of Time

Forewarned is forearmed! Only in this case, it can be more fun. Your kids love gymnastics, karate or swimming and are afraid that they are going to miss out on it in the future? Spend some time together researching their favorite activities in their new area.

Set up a date for contact with friends and family back home. With those closest to us, we have a weekly standing Skype or Whatsapp video call. With others, it's a loose chat group. Find a solution for your family that lets them look to the future, without feeling they must lose the past.

Have a Weekly "Open Emotions Night"

Some kids will try to be brave and keep everything contained inside, in order not to upset their parents. Others will unleash at will, regardless of the time and place. It helps to have a weekly family meeting to discuss all feelings; and to end it on a high note of what you hope will happen and get excited about it. That way, the children learn to express emotions while learning how to create solutions instead of bottling fear. They learn mommy and daddy want to hear and promise not to judge.

It is even better if you could do this during a day, where you have the time to make or order a nice meal and do a family bonding activity afterward.

I recommend continuing the above after the move. It shows how traditions can continue and evolve. You can talk about the highs and lows of the transition, and it will help you bond as a family.

ABOUT SHERRIE MCCARTHY

Sherrie is a writer, mama, bookaholic, and reluctant sailor who traded in motorcycle adventures for mommy adventures on the open seas. Her book *Confessions of a Reluctant Sailor* tells us about her first two years afloat on her boat. *Bust Out of Your Cage:*

Conquering Life's Constraints To Live Your Life On Your Terms helps women build a bridge to a life of joy and passion, rather than obligation and exhaustion.

She co-hosts the Creative Spirits podcast, and she has been a guest on the podcasts Writer On The Road and Those Diner and Motorcycle Guys. Her writing has been featured in *Badassery Magazine, Empowerment 4 Women* as well as Newfoundland and Labrador's online magazine *The Independent*. Currently afloat in the Caribbean, she lives with her family on her boat *Falkor 4.2*.

Website: www.sherriemccarthy.com

Instagram: www.instagram.com/sherriemccarthy

Chapter 17

Our Differences Unite Us
Sangeetha Narayan

It was a beautiful afternoon, the sky clear and blue. Birds were chirping, butterflies were zooming past, and yet my first-born's eyes saw none of it. She came home from school, throwing her backpack in one corner, her eyes threatening to burst any second, her voice shaking, *"I do not like school!"*

I sighed, as I put her backpack where it belonged; got myself busy in the kitchen, hoping that some food in her tummy would soothe her raw nerves and then she could give me more details about her day.

"Don't you want to know why I dislike school?", she came storming into the kitchen.

"Did you get into a fight with someone?", even I could hear the nervousness in my voice.

"My teacher doesn't like me! I think it's because I'm Indian!"

"Why do you think she doesn't like you?", I ask her, trying to buy some time so I could process a response.

"She acts like I don't exist. She never picks me when I raise my hand. When we all are drawing, she will praise my friend's art and completely ignore mine. She hasn't said one positive word about me this entire year!"

I could see that she was feeling miserable about the whole thing. So, I decided to pivot. "Let me tell you about your mom, who had somewhat of a similar experience with her teacher, when she was a little girl. I was a bit on the plumper side. So, all my friends would tease me by calling me 'fatso'. One day, I finally got tired of being treated like this, and I decided to tell my teacher."

"Did the kids get in trouble? Did your teacher yell at the kids?", she asked curiously. I could see that my daughter had forgotten all about her sorrows.

"When I informed my teacher of their misdeeds, she simply laughed. The teacher said they were just telling me the truth." I could still feel the sting of my teacher's laugh, even after so many years.

My little one let out a huge sigh. "So, it's hopeless! Teachers are just mean!"

I directed her by hand to sit on the couch and began gently pattingher hair.

"The point of my story was to tell you that teachers are people too. They can be amazing sometimes and they can make mistakes at other times."

"And if they belong to another community, they can make you feel even more miserable." There was no consoling my daughter.

"If that were true, my teacher should not have been mean as we both were from the same country."

"But they are teachers!", my little one insisted. "They are supposed to know better than us. They are supposed to be teaching us the right path. If we see them being different to children, how do we differentiate between what is right and what is not?"

"They are human!", I replied. "We all have our good days and bad days", I continued gently. "Sometimes it's good to look beyond a person's cultural background or even their age and experience. If we can see them as just human beings, it becomes easier to forgive them for their mistakes."

I let it go at that, and we went on with our day ...

That night, while we were getting ready for bed, my daughter asked, "I didn't understand something. Did you also think my teacher was wrong? You never said anything about what she did."

I knew that question would be coming at some point. "I know that you wouldn't react in this manner unless you really felt something strong. But I also should not comment on something that I did not see. One thing that I would like to say is that it would be smart to separate your teacher's action from her personal background."

I never heard my daughter complain about her teacher after that day. In fact, I have rarely heard her complain about any other teacher or even a friend for that matter. And even if she does have an issue, it is more about what they did or did not do, and less about which culture they belong to.

I personally always remind myself of a famous quote by John Hume, an Irish politician.

"Difference is of the essence of humanity. Difference is an accident of birth and it should therefore never be the source of hatred or conflict. The answer to difference is to respect it. Therein lies a most fundamental principle of peace: respect for diversity."

Listen to the Child

When a child comes home with a complaint, let's take their problems seriously. It is a harsh world out there and parents can prove to be an amazing punching bag. Telling them that they are wrong without completely listening to them, just makes them angrier and less accepting of the world.

101

Face Cultural Differences Head On

Facing cultural differences is given currently. Everywhere they turn, they face this truth - they are different from the people around them. But how they face this difference is an art that can be learned, and parents can be the best teachers. Parents teach children by being what they want their kids to be. When a child observes parents interacting with people across different cultures, they are ready to interact in the same way.

Accept or Not to Accept

When we constantly complain about discrimination, our children have a harder time accepting differences too. Children can sense our insecurities and fears. It is especially important for parents to be aware of the message they are sending to their children. When a parent is less accepting of people's differences, children usually tend to follow them, which only results in trouble.

Transcend Culture

People are meant to be different from each other. However, the difference is not always related to their cultural background. When children learn that we all have our inherent qualities that separate us even as it connects us together, they learn to look beyond a person's culture.

When we learn to separate a person's actions from their culture, that is when we truly learn to accept this diversity and transcend this difference. At the end of the day, the aim is not to just understand different cultures but to know the people that make this culture.

ABOUT SANGEETHA NARAYAN

Sangeetha Narayan is a freelance writer residing in Ellicott City, MD with her husband and two children. A stay-at-home-mom, a volunteer in her children's school, a freelance writer at raising world children, and a book reviewer at online book club, she loves to don many hats at one time. She has also been published on Women's Era and Dimdima. Sangeetha Narayan practices what she likes to call spiritual parenting and encourages other parents to be aware of their thoughts using her writing.

Website: -
https://wordpress.com/view/sursangeet2000.wordpress.com

https://wordpress.com/view/readsangread.wordpress.com

Section III
Building Acceptance

Chapter 18

Learning About the World
Lucretia Marie Anderson

"Understanding languages and other cultures builds bridges. It is the fastest way to bring the world closer together and to Truth. Through understanding, people will be able to see their similarities before differences."
— Suzy Kassem

Walking among the rows of flowers and vegetables growing tall from the fertile soil, my daughter skipped along with her classmates, counting in numbers I couldn't quite comprehend. I was merely a background player, anyway, acting as a chaperone. Her teacher, Shih-laoshi, trailed closely behind her students pointing out various plants and calling out their names in Mandarin Chinese. My daughter and her friends repeated the words effortlessly, now accustomed to the sounds since they had already been part of the immersion program at her school for the better part of the year.

My 1st grader smiled easily as she soaked in both the sunshine and the beauty of her teacher's native tongue, in a brand-new way. Not only was her intellectual curiosity nourished by the Chinese Immersion program, but her ability to see the world through the lens of another culture and language was invaluable. She was being enriched by learning about the customs and traditions of Chinese heritage as well.

When I was a child, I loved the Capital Children's Museum. My mother would take us there often. I remember specifically being fond of the printing press (I have always loved words), and a little area where you could learn about Mexican culture in a little Adobe house, creating tortillas from ground corn. I was just fascinated with getting to explore a culture outside of my own, even if it was in the simplest of ways.

I would eventually often visit the museums of the Smithsonian Institution in Washington, DC as a student and with my family. As an adult, it was an absolute dream to get to work there and help bring a vast number of diverse cultures to children of all ages, through the museum programs and performances at the Smithsonian's Discovery Theater. We were able to expose countless children to our programs, which ranged from in exhibit storytellers, to music and dance performances, puppetry and plays from across the globe.

Learning about the world involves actively engaging with the people of other lands. Immersing ourselves in the stories, food, and arts of those lands is an incredibly powerful tool for understanding one's place as a global citizen.

It is difficult for children to understand that there is a world outside of themselves without experiencing it in some form. Nothing can replace having children interact with the people and affects that are indigenous to a region different from their own. Of course, reading about the world can help to develop interest and even wanderlust. But taking a step into someone else's realm and attempting to see the world through their lens, is truly transformative.

My mother worked for the State Department and traveled abroad several times when I was a child. I loved the stories, pictures, and souvenirs she brought back from Egypt, Thailand, and Ghana. I did not go abroad myself until I was in my 20's, but from my early childhood experiences, I developed a strong desire to learn about the world and make connections.

When I did finally get the opportunity to travel to France and Poland in my early 20's, it was both exhilarating and frightening. By the time I went to Argentina the following year, I was a little more at ease with getting my bearings in a foreign land. As a young adult, I had already developed such a strong sense of what I thought the world to be. I was gob smacked to discover that the people who I thought would not be open, were actually welcoming and eager to share who they were.

As we grow older, I believe it gets harder and harder to step out of our comfort zone and be willing to learn about new people and places.

This is one of the many reasons my good friends, educator, and travel bloggers - Terri Muuss and Matt Pasca, take their two boys on a trip outside of the United States, every year during the Winter Holidays. For years, the philosophy has been to give their children the gifts of experiences, instead of material items. They want their children to be world citizens, who are compassionate and empathetic human beings, and who can learn to adapt wherever they are. In a travel blog post about parents who question traveling with young children - because they either won't remember the trip or who will be too impatient with traveling, Matt wrote:

"Today, when we ask Atticus, now 11, and Rainer, 13, if they recall some of those early trips and destinations, they often do not. Their brains remember, though, as neuropathways are etched by early experiences to form the people we become as fully conscious children and adults. Despite not recalling our early adventures, both boys became fully accustomed to travel and all that goes with it.

So many parents have complained to us that, by the time THEY are ready to travel with their children (because now they will "remember it" and the money won't be "wasted") their KIDS aren't ready for travel. They whine in the car, on the plane, and absolutely do not appreciate the process of being pushed out of their comfort zone. We say: all the more reason not to wait."

Allowing children to be open to the world around them takes an intentional and conscious effort. There are several things that you can do as a parent of young children, whether you can travel with them to explore the world or not.

Diversify Consumption

Visiting your library to check out movies, books, and music; hearing a storyteller; seeing other cultural programming - will all go a long way to foster global awareness. My children and I love to watch foreign language films, to learn more about another culture; or listen to world music to hear the rhythm and cadence of folks from around the world.

Host Multicultural Family Dinners

My good friend, Kathryn, is a huge proponent of gathering people from many cultures at her home, to share in a meal and learn from and about each other. We bring our kids and a dish and simply enjoy each other's company and stories. Building relationships across cultures in this way is a powerful way to truly understand one another.

Visit Cultural Museums

Look for those who will expose your children not only to works of art, but manners, customs, and artifacts from that region and places abroad. Pay careful attention to the cultural education programs that museums offer.

Attend Heritage Festivals

Being immersed in the food, music, dance, and folk arts and crafts, often present at heritage festivals, is a wonderful way to allow young children to experience other customs present in the world around them.

Enroll in an Immersion Program

This allows children to learn from teachers who are usually native speakers, who are not only fluent in the language but in the customs and traditions of those places as well.

Travel Abroad with Your Children

If you have the means, not only are you exposing your children to far off lands but you are getting them accustomed to travel itself. This may prove difficult at first, but the rewards will far outway the pains. My friend and coworker, Lauren Jones, who travels with her now 2 and 5 year olds to Spain every year says, *"The sooner you expose them to traveling and seeing the world, the better it is, before the idea that their existence is the only kind is ingrained in their brains."*

Engaging children with learning about the world in multi-faceted ways, during their early development, will be so beneficial to them as adults who can open themselves up to others.

ABOUT LUCRETIA MARIE ANDERSON

Lucretia is a mother of two, writer, educator, life coach and theatre artist who currently resides in Richmond, Virginia. She is a former arts and cultural education administrator for the Smithsonian Institution's Discovery Theatre and the Folger Shakespeare Library in Washington, DC. She has been a middle school teacher of English and Theatre and has written for *Richmond Mom's Blog* and a compendium on Arts Integration for Intellect Books.

Lucretia is the founder of Joyful Muse Coaching, a service dedicated to transformational life coaching, mindfulness training, and parenting coaching. She has written performance pieces for *If You Could See Me*, a project dedicated to raising awareness and advocacy around mental health issues and is an advocate for adolescent mental wellness and LGBTQ youth. Lucretia is passionate about empowering others, especially children, to use their voices through theatre arts and cultivating self-compassion through mindfulness practice. She spends most of the time reading, performing, or taking the family on various adventures.

Website: www.joyfulmusecoaching.com

Instagram: Instagram.com/lucretianspires

Chapter 19

Incorporating Grandparents'
Parenting Techniques
Sneha Jhanb

*"Young people need something stable to hang on to —
a culture connection, a sense of their own past, a hope
for their own future. Most of all, they need what
grandparents can give them."*
- Jay Kesler

One of the things that I am not very happy about, as a parent raising world children, is keeping my kids miles and miles away from their grandparents. Now this is of course not because I want them away, but because of the choice we have made as adults to stay in the USA. We hope to enrich ourselves with different cultures far away from our own country.

Grandparents played an important role in my life as I grew up. My *Aba* (father's father) lived with us. He died when I was 22. I do not have any memory of life growing up, without him being in the picture.

My mother's parents would come visit us during our exams so that my sister and I had added emotional support. And then they stayed with us during the summer holidays. I cannot remember one single *Diwali* holiday or summer holiday or exam without my *Aji* and *Aba*.

Grandparents bring a whole different world that our parents do not provide us. The world where adults spoil children rotten!

Now when it comes to my children, they get to visit their grandparents once a year for some time, but often it can be two years or more without seeing them.

I was grateful to have both my mother and mother-in-law visit us for an extended time during the birth of both my children. When I became a parent, I realized there is a complicated side to seeing a grandparent in action. Especially, when the grandchild is your kid, and the grandparent is your parent or in law.

The relationship is delicate and if not handled carefully, there can be so many misunderstandings between the people we love and care for.

When it comes to multicultural parenting and adding complexity of grandparents from our culture to the mix, things can get tangled quick.

The Pressure of Being a Multicultural Newbie Parent

When you are a new parent in a new country, it is natural to be influenced by local culture. Being a new parent already means you are extra careful about everything - the way you hold your child, the way you use the carseat, the way your child behaves in the society, everything matters.

When our parents (the grandparents) enter the picture, they have a clear picture of wanting to help but they have their own cultural map and lens.

For example, they might not be used to car seats. When your baby cries in the car, they might make you take him/her out in the moving car because they cannot handle their cries, and that is not what they did with us when we were young. They will probably find it hard to grasp the severity of this situation when it comes to following the law as well as risking your child's life.

They slept next to you till you were an adult. They will probably be totally against you keeping your child in a different room when he/she is a baby. They might be used to bathing little children daily but sometimes in cold climates you do not need to bathe a baby often. They are used to having morning baths but you are giving baths in the evening.

Naturally, they will have things to say about it and they will try to make you understand their point of view.

Apart from the daily upbringing, there are also other rituals and superstitions that you might not think are as important as they are for them. For example, the baby's first solid food is a big ceremony in some cultures, and you are so eager to feed the baby food that you totally did not wait till the ceremony.

Maybe you are totally into sharing your child's pictures everywhere, but they might believe this will bring evil eye upon the child and put a black mark on the child to avoid that.

There are little differences and then there are larger ones. The grandparents do not understand that their grandchild does not belong to the same culture as theirs. My origin is Indian. My kids look Indian BUT their behavior and ways are far from Indian. They identify themselves as Americans when asked. It is hard for some grandparents to grasp this fact.

The pressure is now on us parents - to deal with the culture and expectations of raising kids today, versus the culture and expectations that we were brought up in; and to be able to blend it in a perfect way that does not alienate anyone, and still ticks all the boxes that we want as parents for our children.

How Do We Then Relate with Grandparents of This Generation?

The truth is this is probably the first worldwide generation of grandparents that has to deal with this issue of multiculturalism. We forget that they are also learning the world from a multicultural point of view.

They were brought up in a society, where they saw their grandparents giving their parents advice, and their parents taking their advice without asking questions or raising eyebrows. Their parents did not have as many raised eyebrows from their children, as much as they are getting used to getting from us.

The truth is we all have our own set of worries and problems. When we look to our parents, we always look for support. When it comes to multicultural parenting, the support needed is also mental and emotional. And sometimes due to differences of opinions, the very support system that we look forward to becomes a hindrance.

As much as it is the job of us as parents to understand our parents' point of view, it is that much more important for today's grandparents to understand their children. They should try and understand the new ways of their children's' lives better, to create harmony and peace in their grandchild's upbringing.

When it comes to relating and dealing with differences, I believe in clear and conscious communication. It might feel unnecessary and an added burden but giving a clear idea of where you are coming from as a parent, what society norms are, what you are aiming to achieve as a parent and being confident in your shoes, is what it takes to start the conversation. When you are starting a communication, it also means to listen and understand your parents' point of view and where they are coming from.

If you must, you should keep disciplining and sharing cultural values as a 'parents' job', and the extra support, love and nurturing that kids most need as a 'grandparents job'.

When we consciously do not overstep the boundaries of parenting, it helps to decrease the risk of getting agitated. **It means grandparents being more open to having this communication with their children, and understanding their unique pain of raising children in societies that do not look, talk, walk, or behave like the ones they brought their children up in.**

How Do We Live Far Away but Still Keep the Connection Close?

In our case, the children's grandparents live in a different country. It is not many times that we face differences of opinions. But what is more of a problem is that the connection between the grandparents and grandkids can be lost or not be the same as we had with our grandparents.

A great way of keeping our children connected with their grandparents is through technology. My older son has full liberty to call his grandparents on his own, whenever he feels like (as long as he understands the time difference and does not disturb their sleep). That way he knows he has extra emotional support, if he ever needs it. It also helps the grandparents have great communication with my children and helps build their own rapport.

With distance, relations do get tough to maintain. But these are our parents, who brought us up and the younger ones are their grandchildren. **It is only fair to not let any differences of opinion amongst adults hurt relationships of grandparents and grandchildren in the long haul.** A little mindfulness, open communication and technology goes a long way.

ABOUT SNEHA JHANB

Sneha is the founder of Stress Less With Sneha J and owner of Prosperous Financial Services, LLC. Sneha is an Industrial Engineer turned Certified Mindfulness Teacher, Sound Healing Practitioner and Financial Professional. She helps families connect with their financial and emotional wellbeing and helps achieve stress free prosperity. Her upcoming book Stress Free Prosperity provides real life and simple strategies for the same. She is passionate about connecting consciously in this world and wants to share these values with her 2 boys.

Website: https://stresslesswithsnehaj.com

Instagram: Instagram.com/stresslesswithsnehaj

Chapter 20

Building Cross Cultural Friendships
Nupur Biswal

About a week into middle school, a friend of my elder daughter told her that, *"she needs more brown friends."* Although this statement may have seemed like a harmless joke between two Middle School South Asian girls to anyone, its underlying meaning and implications were a red flag to me.

Sure, it is refreshing and heartwarming to be with people who come from a similar background as you. It makes you feel as though you belong because you are surrounded by people who remind you of your home and family. However, if your need to be with others who are like you, reduces your ability to go beyond racial divides and befriend people from a variety of backgrounds...then there is a problem!

Many of us tend to specifically seek out friendships with people of the same race and restrict our children's friendship too. It is a natural inclination — the issue, however, rises when people become so focused on having friends of the same race that they are indifferent or even subconsciously opposed to the possibility of being friends with someone of a different race.

Why are Multicultural Friendships Important?

"Experiences and values are not restricted by race and neither should our friendships."

We live in a diverse country that is composed of many people of different ethnicities. Learning about different cultures and values is imperative to having an open mind and understanding the world around us from different people's perspectives. When we only associate with people who think and act like us, we deprive ourselves of these experiences.

"Friends Are Families We Choose" – Edna Buchman

Friends make great teachers. You can learn - different languages; other cultures; a variety of experiences that people of different races and religions offer; different traditions; and differing viewpoints get imbibed just by spending quality time with someone from a different background. Even more so, you can teach them things as well. All it takes is one discussion with a friend, and you can gain so much information on a specific culture.

When you make friends with people from different cultures or religions, you will soon see that many stereotypes proved to be false.

Having a diverse group of friends can teach you how to accept people who have different views than you, and to learn to seek out different ideas. Having friends from different backgrounds will also teach you to love people for who they are. You will become aware of your own subconscious prejudices and be forced to address them. In addition, you will develop a connection to people, who have different struggles of their own. When it is a friend that has faced discrimination, you are more likely to become aware of how the discrimination affects them on a deeper level. You will have a personal connection to it and be more invested in solving issues than others.

Why is It Important to Make Multicultural Bonds When Children are Young?

First, research shows that among adults, same-race friendships are more prevalent than cross-race friendships. Research conducted by The Human Psychology Department Of Yale University shows that in a group of 10,000 people composed of various age groups, 41% of children aged 5-9 years old wanted to make friends with other children irrespective of their races. Whereas 22% of children aged 10-16 years old showed their willingness in cross-cultural friendships. Surprisingly, only 12% of adults were interested in the same.

Hence, we can clearly see that children are unbiased when it comes to making friends. They usually do not judge children by the color of the skin, rather they choose their friends depending on their common interests or likings. But gradually with age this quality changes; so as responsible parents, we need to preserve these unbiased attitudes of our children by encouraging cross-cultural friendships since childhood.

How Can We Develop Cross Cultural Bonds?

There are many opportunities for children to find more diverse friends. For instance -

Schools

Schools are often one of the first places that children interact with peers from outside their familiar groups, and this opportunity to interact is important. These days schools are becoming more diverse, so children are getting more opportunities to make friendships with children from other countries than before. But simply having a diverse group of children in a school does not mean that the children will form cross-friendships.

Even with the opportunity to mix, close cross-group friendships have been found to remain relatively uncommon, are less durable, and decline with age. As an involved parent, you can play a greater role in your child's life. So if your child finds a new friend who is from a different country than yours, be excited about his new friend! Your child is always looking to you for cues on how to think or feel about things. Seeing you be at ease and enthusiastic about their new classmate, will set the tone for how they approach him or her.

Discuss where the new friend is from and find it on the map. Just this small step of seeing their two home countries on a map, can help to bring something familiar to mind, when approaching a new culture. It removes an element of the unknown.

Learn a couple of phrases from his language and encourage your child to smile and say hello to his new friend in his mother tongue. As Mother Teresa once said, *"Every time you smile at someone, it is an action of love, a gift to that person, a beautiful thing."* So never underestimate the power of a smile!

Another benefit of learning a new language will be that your child will relate to what it might be like, to be immersed in a new language and unable to understand others or to communicate. It can be frustrating sometimes, but an understanding and compassionate friend can prove to be helpful in such situations, so try to be that friend.

Libraries and Parks

Local libraries and parks often host events to celebrate a range of holidays relevant from other countries. These events, along with the stories read and games played there, can be great icebreakers for building friendships. There may also be groups that meet regularly at a local park or library that focus on a certain language or culture or dance forms from another country. Ask your local librarian or park ranger for details. Participating in such activities also help building cross cultural friendships.

Cultural Festivals

Check out community calendars, local websites, and other sources for information on ethnic festivals, holiday celebrations, and cultural activities. Attending these can be a lot of fun and offer new and interesting games, crafts, food, and other activities to add to your family's repertoire. Ideally, you will also meet some families there whose kids hit it off with yours and can provide them with new ways of viewing the world.

Sport Teams

Depending on where you live, immigrant families may regularly get together to play their national sports. Such groups are generally welcoming to local families who want to join in. In addition to learning how to play a new sport, you are also likely to learn a good deal about the culture from which it comes. Team spirit is a great way to build connections within people from diverse walks of life.

Pen-Pal Programs

The Internet has transformed traditional pen-pals into electronic pen-pals or "ePals." And while there will be no more exotic stamps and fascinating stationery arriving from far away, gone, too, is the necessity of waiting weeks for a response. Parents should exercise caution and focus on sites that do not require any personal information from your child and monitor with whom they email or chat. Having said that, there are still many rewarding sites worth looking at, including Students of the World, ePals Global Community, and A Girl's World.

If you cannot find a group to join in your area that is dedicated to international and cross-cultural exchange, consider starting one!

Of course, friendships must be organic and not forced. But if your lifestyle permits, try stretching yourself and encouraging your child to add more diverse and multicultural friendships to their existing mix. *Your children can learn many great life lessons from dealing on their own terms with children from radically different cultures and backgrounds, whether they are kids from faraway places or kids who look, and act differently and yet live in the same town.*

ABOUT NUPUR BISWAL

Nupur Biswal is an ex-software engineer turned STEM educator & Marketing and Social Content Creator for multiple companies. She lives in San Antonio Texas, with her husband and two children. She is an active member of PTO of her children's school and involved in various after school programs. She also volunteers in her local museum and libraries to raise awareness for reading and STEM education among children. She is a freelance writer and a book reviewer with 'Readers Favorite', 'Multicultural Children's Book Day' & 'Bookstagram Choice Awards'. So far her articles are published in Parent & Kids -North Mississippi, Think Fun and Testing Mom to name a few. Nupur practices what she likes to call mindful parenting. She believes in simple & powerful solutions for raising creative, engaged and happy kids in today's hectic world. Her motto is more connection & less conflict with her children and she believes in spreading her knowledge and experiences through her parenting articles.

Facebook: https://www.facebook.com/Lovemygam/

Instagram: https://instagram.com/nupurbiswal

Chapter 21

Fitting in After a Move
Sybil Jones

M y husband is a US Naval Officer, and we average a move every 2 to 3 years. Yes, we move very often!

Our children, now tweens and teens, were very vocal about our latest move, where our family should live and which school they should attend.

Let me rewind a bit and talk about how we adjust to moving every couple of years, and how our children have adapted to fitting in with new peers frequently.

Most of our moves have been within the United States, but we have also lived and traveled abroad. We moved to Japan when our kids were 3, 5, and 7. Our school-aged kids attended the military school on base, while our preschooler attended an English-speaking Japanese preschool. That was the best of both worlds for her. Yes, we had a preschooler translate for us from time to time. There is no shame in our game!

While living in Japan, we had an enjoyable experience learning about the Japanese culture, building new friendships and exploring a whole new world.

Was it scary when we first arrived?

Yes! But we took a deep breath, walked out of little America (the military base), made every attempt to learn and speak the language, and enjoyed every moment in another country. We traveled to a few other countries and enjoyed the experiences there as well.

I did not pay much attention to how the kids responded to or adjusted with moves, until it was time to move from our duty station that followed Japan. By this point, the kids were in 7th, 5th, and 3rd grades. We moved to Hawaii the day after Christmas, in the middle of the school year.

Our youngest kids didn't mind, but our eldest had established strong friendships; Friendships that she wasn't ready to leave.

How do you handle when a child does not want to leave friends? What do you say? Honestly, I did not know. I told her friends' parents; they were all welcome to visit us anytime.

Luckily, all three kids made friends quickly. For hubby and I, we moved into a neighborhood where we had friends. Friends we made while stationed in Japan. Everyone was happy!

People ask how we break the news to our kids about each new move. Ok, this may sound horrible, but it has worked for us over the past 15 years with children in this military life. We tell them we are moving! The delivery is very matter of fact, and we carry on. We handle deployments or anytime husband goes TDY (travels for work) the same way. There's no big deal about it, no count down for returns, etc. It's part of our lives, and we roll with it!

That was until the day I found out we were leaving Hawaii. Oh! WAIT! The news came through the door, 18 months early. We had to move again! We had to pack up and move on 10-months-orders.

We are now moving a rising high school freshman, 7th grader, and 5th grader. Moving these ages for one school year is insane! I knew they were going to flip.

When we broke the news, they were ok with it and ready to go. For our eldest, she was going to move back closer to where friends she made between 5th and 7th grade lived. Trust me, they take every opportunity to meet up.

I will be honest here. I had a full-on tantrum about this move. It wasn't about leaving Hawaii; it was about the timing. There were trips planned for island hopping and a few plans for family and friends to visit. But this is what we do...we adjust. We adjust because this is the life we live, and I have loved it from day one!

I vowed not to make a huge deal about our moves, when we had children. This was because we felt that making it a big deal would only cause them stress and worry. This practice has helped our kids throughout the many moves they have endured. And it helped them handle my tantrum. So, after our kids stared at me like I was a crazy lady, and told me to *"Get my life together"*, I dusted myself off and got it together!

Ok, so as I promised, we are almost back to the present day. Remember, I mentioned how our kids are now vocal about where they live and the school they attend? I am getting to that here...

As we searched for homes, our children requested some input on the area we lived and the school they attended. They wanted a neighborhood and school that offered diversity and lots of it. They wanted to see the world within their front door. So, we made that happen!

We moved to our new home and school started the following month. The first day was a bust: maneuvering the halls, finding classes, lunchtime. Oh, boy! Lunchtime. Sitting alone at lunch and roaming the halls lost. Not a great combination!

Ok, no biggie. Go back for day two, and it will be ok. Day two was not any better. Ok, this will be fine! But if you have teenagers, we already know the world is coming to an end at this point.

This was new territory for me; the kids had never complained in the past. I was never told that it was our fault about having them leaving friends and having to start over time and time again.

Ok, pause. Yes, I had to have a long talk with myself to get my mind right. I wanted to yell, but I knew emotions were high, feelings were being shared, and the truth was coming out.

I could not burden my husband with the long talks and frustration taking place after school. He was in school himself! He was trying to get settled and getting to know the classmates, who he would be working on projects with and traveling with.

Our youngest child had none of these concerns. She was in the 5th grade and living her best life. All was great in her world, even with the little boy she beefed with from day one. We later figured out what was going on there.

Our middle daughter (7th grader) was slowly finding her groove. She admitted that the alternate-day schedule had one day better than the other, but she was ok.

Week two was still a hot mess for our freshman. She was still trying to figure out where her group was. By this point, her 7th grade sister (they attend the same school and ride the same bus) and I told her to relax. Sit with the girls you met on the first day and have small talk. Ask simple questions about schedules, ask if they are new to the school, talk about the summer, etc. Just be yourself!

You excel when you are being yourself! Trust me, you will find your groove and your people.

Finally, the day came when everyone walked through the door happy! I heard about receiving compliments and about the numerous voices of hearing hello, etc.

Each child came home talking about the exchange of phone numbers, snaps, etc.

Yes, I told you so! The moment you relax and be yourself, everyone sees your light and is drawn to it.

"Beauty begins the moment you decide to be yourself." – Coco Chanel

You already know that I could not let the attitude and complaining go without questioning.

All three kids said moving every few years was easy for them when they were young. Now that they are getting older and friendships are formed by their choice vs. hanging out because parents are friends, it is harder to let go and trust new people to enter their world.

They shared that they have been upset in the past about moving. They never shared it because they knew how much stress we were dealing with, in preparation for the move. And they knew it was part of their lives with a father in the military. Even though they were a bit vocal with this latest move, they understand and appreciate the lesson we have taught them, when it comes to moving every couple of years. They appreciate the lesson of always knowing who they are, being who they are, and loving who they are.

Never try to fit in. Always Be Yourself and true friendships will form!

ABOUT SYBIL JONES

Sybil is a Navy wife of 18 years, mother of three (tween and teen girls), and owner of a silly little Maltese named Carlos. She's a graduate of The University of Memphis, where she received her B.B.A. in Logistics and Marketing. She's currently working on her

Ph.D. from The University of Life. Her passion is to empower others in life with her message of Know You Be You Love You®. You can also find her having fun at her site, Mamas and Coffee®. She is also the owner of Sybil Talks. A platform promoting self-love and body image (from the skinny perspective). She is the host of Milspouse Conversations™, an online space and monthly virtual meetups for military spouses to have real, raw and supportive conversations about military spouse life.

Website: www.mamasandcoffee.com

Facebook: www.facebook.com/momjonz

Chapter 22

Comparing Old and New Heritage
Jewel Eliese

"A people's relationship to their heritage is the same as the relationship of a child to its mother."
- John Henrik Clark

On a nine-hour flight with children, you may expect the worst. Crying, whining, feet pumping, a toddler head sleeping on your lap (when you only wish to use the too-tiny bathroom), but our flight went well. My little humans even managed to sleep, which meant some shuteye for me.

Yet, those four hours of rest still do not prepare you for the arrival to a foreign country. You walk off the plane to find everything different.

Everything.

Including heritage, which gets interesting when you have children. There were a few heritage and cultural differences we noticed and remembered on the recent trip abroad. And it had me wondering, is learning about culture and heritage good for kids? For us as parents?

Or were these differences too overwhelming? While every country has its positives and negatives there were a few things for my children, and for me at times, that seemed overwhelming in the moment, but never wrong. Simply different. And *different* is beautiful.

The Bathrooms

My four-year-old daughter needed to use the restroom when we first arrived at the airport, and her comment made me smile. She said, "It stunk". While this is, of course, not an uncommon occurrence for public restrooms, I remember thinking the same thing when I lived in Ukraine.

Granted my little girl is from a small town and is not used to big city life, but even bathrooms are different when you're across the sea, and one of the first changes someone tends to notice.

House Shoes and Bundling Up

Ukraine is cold. While not as frigid as my ND home temperatures, the air is more humid leaving your skin hydrated but freezing. Many homes have wooden or tiled floors, which lead to chilly toes. This is why you'll find many Ukrainians wearing house shoes, which for someone who is not used to putting on other people's shoes, was strange.

You wear the house shoes, so you don't get sick from the cold, a fear passed on from generations. Staying warm is part of their heritage. Even now when we are at home, Ukrainian Grandma and Grandpa bundle up my children well, until they end up looking like the little brother from the movie *A Christmas Story*.

Superstitions

If you're American, you know that a black cat walking across your path is bad luck. Same if you walk under a ladder. Broken mirror? Seven years of it.

But there were times living abroad, I felt like I could not go anywhere without doing something that would stir up bad or good omens.

Such as,

- Cold feet? You will not be able to have children one day or will get sick.

- Whistling in the house? You will be poor.

- Purse on the floor? It will be empty.

And the same goes for when you become a parent. The heritage of superstition follows through. You may notice a child wearing a necklace or string around their wrist that is red. This is because the parents are protecting their child from 'bad eyes' i.e., people who would steal the child's energy, leaving them with a headache or ill.

Baptism

We visited Ukraine this time for a joyful reason, a new baby. My husband was to be the Godfather. The baby was gorgeous. I wanted to hold her, take pictures, and show her off to the world like much of our American culture does.

But that was not so easy.

In the states, we tend to have a large group of people show up to the hospital after a birth. It's a celebration for all, though the parents are not dressed in their best and may be feeling out of sorts.

But the old heritage is different.

Instead, only the parents stay at the hospital. No one else arrives with balloons and gifts to the room. Immediate relatives wait until the baby and parents are home. The rest of the family wait until the day of the baptism, when the baby will finally be saved, protected, and ready for the world.

Holidays

One of which was the holidays. Each felt like Thanksgiving with family celebrating, smiling, drinking, and eating traditional foods. There are so many holidays, even a name day (kind of like in *Game of Thrones*). Some people joke that the reason there are so many holidays, is so there is a reason to eat, and drink.

But I found the feasts with family and friends, and to see each gather around the table to be a lovely tradition. One that I hope to raise my own children with.

Growing in spite of ...

All these differences in heritage can leave a person feeling confused, and at times upset. You can feel alone. Lost. And like a red tack in a drawer of white ones – you are different. Glaring and sticking out.

Turn this around and you will see foreigners here feeling this same. Each culture and heritage is different, which makes others feel out of sorts; yet all cultures have positives.

In the end, the old and new heritages showed me and my children that we each need to take a moment to learn about global culture. Take the good and learn from the rest.

We become better people when we understand our global family. When our children understand culture and heritage, our future brightens. It does not overwhelm children but enlightens them.

I've found myself becoming a better person. I can empathize with someone who is immigrating, the nine-hour flight and how different everything is, even the bathroom.

But the best part is, I can see how my kids treat others because of learning about heritage and culture as well. They are more kind, sensitive, and seem to understand others in their daily lives.

Therefore, it is so important we each take a chance to discover cultures, near and far.

Yet, this was only our experience, our subjective perspective. My own life experiences and the places I visited in Ukraine played a part in my views. You need to discover it for *yourself.*

Which is why I challenge you to try these few ideas and see how other cultures and heritages change your world, and your children's.

Talk

You do not need to travel far. You can do this by talking with your neighbor, who just moved from across the world, or even from another state.

Pals

We live in an amazing time where you can meet people from all over the globe, while sitting in your pajamas. Use your online resources to make incredible friends from everywhere, and then stay in touch with them. Like Aditi, the author of this book, and I have done.

You will not regret it.

Turn the Page

The last challenge is one you have already taken, when you picked up this book. You care enough about culture and teaching your children that you're ready to absorb what knowledge you can. Congratulations.

So, your last challenge is to continue reading. Turn, click, or flip to the next page.

We will see you there.

ABOUT JEWEL ELIESE

Jewel has been published on Scary Mommy, is an Amazon best-selling author and ghostwriter, and is part of the leadership team at The Write Practice Pro. Jewel runs on lukewarm coffee and baby kisses and she believes every mom can write.

Website: https://jeweleliesewriter.com/

Instagram: https://www.instagram.com/jeweleliese_writer/

Chapter 23

Teaching Kids
About Civic Responsibility
Ronda Bowen

Last summer, I stepped up to help lead a Girl Scouts troop. Girl Scouts provides a venue for a core troop of girls, to get together to experience the outdoors, take on service opportunities, learn, and lead.

While immersing myself fully in all things Girl Scouts, one of the things I learned about was the "take action project" that accompanies Journey awards – and ultimately that drives the Girl Scout Bronze, Silver, and Gold Awards. The idea is that troop members find a need in their community that they can provide a sustainable solution to. Some troops plant gardens, some find ways to provide clean water, some build little free libraries. The purpose of the project, and the higher awards, is to teach Girl Scouts the importance of civic engagement, while also teaching important leadership skills.

I have a long history of civic engagement and volunteer work. I even founded a website devoted to community involvement and activism, and I believe that we all must make the world we live in a better place. I believe that the greatest demonstration of love for one's country is engagement within our communities.

"In the face of impossible odds, people who love this country can change it." – President Barack Obama

It's no surprise then, that I feel how vital it is to teach children about civic responsibility & duty to the community. In scouting organizations around the world, one of the tenants of the promise said at every meeting and event is some form of dedicating one's self to community service. This is all great – but how do we teach children to commit to being civically engaged?

First, We Teach What Civic Duty Is

The best way is to model the behaviors we want to see. We need to ourselves be civically engaged in our communities.

Watching parents volunteer for organizations – from youth sporting organizations to organizations helping with various causes to volunteering for political campaigns – is beneficial. Taking children when you go vote helps your children see voting as a central part of life.

Make sure your kids know about their local community. Early adventures can include taking advantage of your local police and fire departments' open houses or offers of tours. Take your child with you to the post office. When you renew your license, let your children wait with you. Many communities have events where the mayor is there. Go to them.

Don't be afraid of letting your children talk to the mayor if there's an opportunity to do so. Teach them about the elections and what the three branches of government are and what they do.

Then, Get Out There and Participate – With the Kids

Within Girl Scouts, we have our troop members get out there and get involved with service projects from the time they are 5 years old and in Kindergarten. There's no reason you have to wait until kids are "old enough" to help them participate in things like coat drives, handing out "I Voted" stickers, or even helping to plan and plant a community garden. Children have an amazing ability to live up to – and surpassing – our expectations.

By having children get involved with their communities – through volunteer work, through following you to the polls, through coming up with sustainable ways to make a difference in their schools, clubs, and communities – we are planting the seeds for a life of community service and community engagement.

Let Your Child Start to Take the Lead

When you raise a child, who is civically engaged from an early age, that child is going to start to see areas in your community that could use some help. Write those ideas down. Some of these ideas may be more viable than others.

For example, if you frequent a walking path, your child may become aware of the trash that has been left behind. Instead of saying *"we should pick up that trash"*, ask your child what he or she thinks should be done about it. Your child will likely say exactly that or maybe he or she may have also noticed a lack of trash bins and point out that there need to be more of those available.

Letting your child take the lead is vital. It may certainly be easier to guide your child and tell him or her what needs to be done. However, allowing the child to come up with the solution serves two functions.

1) It allows your child to realize that he or she has the power to be part of a solution.

2) It allows your child to develop critical steps toward independence by building confidence.

Helping Your Child Use His or Her Voice without Taking Over

So, your child has identified a problem – trash – and a solution – more trash bins. Because the walking path is owned by the city, you can't just go and buy more trash bins and place them where they're needed.

There are other questions that need to be answered. How many bins are needed and where are the best locations for them? How will they be maintained? Do we need to secure them in any way due to our area's weather patterns? Who will empty them? How much will it cost? How do we get this approved?

In Girl Scouts, we are told when having our troop members prepare to take up action projects – or in this case, what might be a Bronze Award for a troop of 4th and 5th graders, that the girls need to do the work. Now, a 5 or 6-year-old is likely too young to find out who to contact. But you can certainly sit with your child and go through the steps of finding out who to contact while talking through what you are doing. An older child may be able to carry out this step with minimal supervision.

Your role in this situation is to be a facilitator, not the person carrying it out. Consider allowing your child to contact the person in charge of maintaining walking paths in your community, after having your child rehearse what he or she may say.

It's important to teach children to use their voice in this manner. As a parent, I know how tempting it is to rush in and want to handle the various steps of a project your child has come up with – but we mustn't step in unless a step cannot be completed without help.

Think of it like bicycle training wheels – we only want those wheels on long enough for the child to develop the confidence needed to try riding without them.

Keeping them on for too long is harmful and creates too much dependence on them for balance. When they are finally removed, the child may have a dip in confidence, when balancing is more difficult than he or she thought it would be.

A Note About Community Activism

Activism is another crucial part of civic engagement. Many of Girl Scouts' Gold Award recipients take on projects that include an activist component.

Activism is the utilization of campaigning to bring about some change.

Protest can be a form of activism, but so can something like a letter-writing campaign to government representatives - to bring about change.

In our example of maintaining walking paths, perhaps your child has also noticed that many of the paths are inaccessible to those who have disabilities. An activist campaign might include heading to city council meetings to share accessibility concerns, following discussion with the local parks and recreation district.

Civic Engagement Is Vital

Even if your child never takes on a big service project like the walking route's trash bins, make sure your child understands the importance of being civically engaged. This is a critical part of raising a child who is conscious of the needs of others.

It helps children to know that their voice matters, and it helps them to grow into adults who are then engaged in their communities. It also teaches children to identify problems, propose a solution, and take action to implement that solution.

Apathy in young adults when it comes to civic responsibility is a problem in every generation. Upon being asked, while leaving the Constitutional Convention, what sort of government delegates had decided upon, Benjamin Franklin responded,

"A republic, if you can keep it."

Democracy requires that citizens are engaged with their society, that they are speaking up, voting, and participate in ensuring that their communities are taking care of the needs of those living there.

By raising world children who understand the weight of community involvement, we can help ensure that we keep our republic.

ABOUT RONDA BOWEN

Ronda Bowen wears a lot of hats. Ronda runs her own editorial consulting business, a specialty boutique, and three blogs. She leads an active multi-level Girl Scout troop, serves as Fundraising Director for the charity JB Dondolo (just honored by the Dallas chapter of the UN for their work on SDG 6 – Clean Water). She also works with a local branch of the Juvenile Arthritis Foundation to organize their annual Jingle Bell Run. She has a master's degree in philosophy, and publishes articles on social and political philosophy, ethics, what we can learn about ourselves from pop culture, and environmentalism. She has served as Senior Editor for Equanimity Magazine since its inception in 2009, and she is working on launching SNARK! a magazine dedicated to literary fiction, poetry, and snarky social commentary.

Ms. Bowen loves archery, hiking, and kayaking, and being unplugged as much as possible.

Website: http://rondabowen.com

Instagram: https://instagram.com/justasecular

Chapter 24

Infusing New Cultures
Purvi Mangtani

"It is time for parents to teach young people early on that in diversity there is beauty and there is strength."
- Maya Angelou

Are you a parent that questions the readiness of their child to learn about this world and its characteristics? Have you wondered what your child feels when looking at new things? To blend is to grow but, do you worry if it is useful for children to learn early? If yes, then you are not alone.

As you metaphorically walk through the article, you will begin to agree if you are not a believer already, that learning about the differences that co-exist in our society is imperative. It is in the best interest of our children that they learn about diversity, with the support of parents and loved ones or the world unconventionally teaches them anyway.

Experiences are always a boon! Sooner or later, we learn from them.

It can be tricky at times, to raise children in a culturally intertwined world if the importance of differences is not comprehended by ourselves. I learned the significance and beauty of cultural diversity through the experiences I had, and before becoming a parent myself.

I must have been four years old when our caravan of life shifted for the first time, from India to the Middle East. Earlier for my father's employment and later for our better educational privileges, I along with my two siblings toggled between cultures. Although we were young, the cultural tremor was felt.

Back then, most families in India practiced the art of dropping in at their convenience. People did not call before stopping over. They would just appear and leave you grumbling within, for voicing *"No"* upfront was and is unheard of. One entertaining instance from my childhood was seeing our plans getting hijacked by a family of six. The modus operandi must have been to test our hospitality lessons, learned as a vital part of the code of conduct of the *Hindu* Society. In India, there is a strong belief that goes as *'Atithi Devo Bhava'* – The guest is equivalent to God. The bottom line was we had to cancel our plans to satisfy their appetite for tea and snacks. On the other hand, in most Middle East countries people discreetly inquired with prior notification of a possible intrusion on others' privacy. We learned this as well, with bittersweet experiences.

In India, I came from an urban space where co-education was common and life, in general, was more liberal for women. Whereas, in most of the middle east countries, education was still quite distinctly scripted for the female gender. I studied in an all-girls school, and it was awkward. Not that there was anything majorly wrong with it, but it is always enlightening to have a look at life from the male perspective in your formative years.

The day I failed at the interview.

I still recall the day I was denied a job upfront. Commended for my academic and social skills, but what ruined my brilliant profile was the "appearance" criteria. I was not glamorous enough, because in the Middle East, women love to dress prim and proper with dollops of glamor and makeup in place. Imagine speaking for yourself and excitedly underlining all your achievements but not being heard. The fact dawned on me that my grooming skills were not on par with other charming women, regardless of working or not. So it was time to align to variances.

Those times were challenging, but the experiences gained through the moving around, come in handy today. It prepared me to face the more complex and diverse world that we live in now.

Faces will change, but the Mirror of Trials never will.

As an individual, I have braved many social storms and learned the variances between India, the Middle East, and the USA.

Today, I am a mother of two girls, born in the United States of America – the embodiment of ethnic mosaic. My 4-year-old daughter started school early this year. She is already experiencing multi-cultural facets like languages, traditions, cuisines, appearances, music, and even beliefs from different individuals around her. At home, she and her younger sister are gradually learning our family traditions from the *Hindu* culture, for that is an essential part of their being. With all the experiences from my past and the learnings of the present, I hope to pass on wise advice to my children, so they can embrace the multiplicity of cultures.

To accept the dissimilarities and focus on adaptability, it is pivotal to first learn about cultures and the significance of diversity. As you will see below, some ideas have proven helpful in infusing new cultures for my little ones. I hope it does it for you too.

The Best Recitations are in the Memories of the Elders

When my daughters hear fictional as well as real-life stories from their grandparents, we too learn new things every time. They narrate the most incredible stories with characters and attributes like none other.

Keep *"Later"* Aside, Where Your Child's Desire for Knowledge is Concerned

Like any inquisitive child, my daughter currently loves to play the game of the *why's* and *how's*. So, whatever appears different from what we translate or do at home, she will ask right away. I filter the in-depth facts because she is too little to handle the complex data for now. But I enlighten her by underlining the moral highlights, for she is curious to learn at that moment. For instance, Thanksgiving is about being grateful and Christmas is about celebrating the birth of Jesus.

Also, drawing parallels from different cultures could be a prodigious way for children to relate, learn, respect diversity, and become more inclusive in their approach.

For instance, *Hanukkah*, the Jewish festival, and *Diwali* are both known as the festival of lights. Both involve lighting up the home.

Longer Routes Take More Effort but Often Lead to More Scenic Vistas.

In many parts of the world, local festivals or events are celebrated extravagantly. The rituals and preparations are quite visible publicly, thereby making learning relatively easier. For instance, *Diwali* celebrations in India are majestic and flamboyant. In the USA, it is celebrated within parameters as laid out by the local authorities. Similar will be the case with any other festival that is not local to a particular place. So, teaching children about some festivals will need more effort in some parts of the world.

It is beneficial for them to learn about the culture or subcultures, so it is worthy of all efforts. Below is one way of doing it, with an assurance of generating interest in your child.

We all recognize that children hanker for fun and group activities. Assigning tasks relating to the festival and allowing them the opportunity to be creative will accentuate learning. Each year during *Diwali*, we invite my daughter's friends to join us for painting *Diyas* and *Rangoli* making. *Diyas* are oil lamps usually made from clay, with a cotton wick dipped in ghee or vegetable oil. *Rangoli*, on the other hand, is Folk Art from India, which is symbolic of good luck and is typically made on the floor using bright colors. It makes it easier for them to learn about the traditions and activities associated with this *Hindu* festival.

Similarly, we look forward to joining our friends from other cultures/subcultures in their festivals and ceremonial preparations.

For instance, every year, we get the privilege of celebrating *Onam* (a harvest festival), with our *Malayali Hindu* friends in the US. Our friends don their traditional attire; prepare the traditional vegetarian dish - *Onam Sadya* (a multi-course vegetarian meal that features over 24 items on a banana leaf); and arrange *Pookalams* (floral carpets prepared with yellow flowers). The history behind this festival is beautiful, and so are the aesthetic vibes of the *Kerala* culture.

Tip: Be the originator of such learning platforms if you have to, without limiting to any specific ethnicity. The sole drive is to give our children a visual guide to various cultural aspects. As it is said, *"Don't look for a tree to take cover when you can grow one."*

Frequent Playdates for Cross-Cultural Bonds

My older daughter did not start talking like many other kids her age. She was shy and clung onto us no matter what we tried. To add to her difficulties, I delivered her baby sister, so that took me away from her immediate circle of comfort for a short span.

Here's my confession, I like any other parent, struggled for some time to figure an easy aid to this challenge. Until one day, when a girl a year older to my daughter came home to play. That unplanned play date opened doors to so many possibilities for us.

After a couple of playdates within a month, we were able to see miraculous developments.

Interactions and communications while at play can prompt easy learning and mutual respect for each other's social variations. Notching it higher by including children from varied ethnic backgrounds, can help achieve the goal of introducing a new culture to your child.

Your child will get exposure to a wide range of characteristics including language, behavioral patterns, opinions, or beliefs - good and sometimes not so good practices too. That is when appropriate decision-making patterns will evolve. Your child, under your guidance, will learn to pick between the *"Do's & Dont's"* to emulate.

For instance, my daughter displayed the obedience of tidying the space after her playtime since she was two years old and without any hassle. But after a few playdates, we realized reluctance from her because the other kid wouldn't do it. It was discouraged as soon as we noticed, for it is appropriate to teach them discipline and responsibility for their tasks.

You are Constantly Watched

During one of our trips to India, my older daughter saw us touching the feet of elders within family and acquaintances. Amazed by the very sight of this gesture, she could not contain asking about it. We gracefully educated her on an interesting facet of culture and subcultures within India. *Hindus* believe in bowing down and touching the feet of their elders to indicate respect for the age, experience, and wisdom of the other person.

It is wise to generate similar platforms for our children to observe and learn by asking questions. For instance, host or participate in themed parties, where you can don a traditional attire or voice briefly about a country's cuisine, history, festivals, languages, and even sports. It can be quite entertaining as well as educating.

Since all the focus will be on YOU, you can wisely sashay with new concepts for young minds. At a similar party, my daughter was thrilled by looking at someone dressed in a *Kimono* (the Japanese traditional garment).

Be Glad THAT Dinosaurs Couldn't Read

It cannot be said to what extent reading can lead to adaptation, but it certainly helps. Good reads will usher your children to the world full of imaginations, where there is respect for one and all.

Create a small library at home or have access to the nearby library; either way but have one reading utopia for sure. It's an extraordinary way of introducing your child to reading a variety of books from different cultures and backgrounds. Some of the books to illustrate are *Babies Around the World* and *Ten Tiny Babies.* These illustrated books follow the day-to-day activities of a bunch of multi-ethnic babies and are enjoyable due to their colorful presentations.

Also, when playing the role of a storyteller at your child's bedtime, read or weave stories not confining the characters to any specific ethnicity. For instance, the children's book *'Say Goodnight'* is a short and adorable bedtime story, highlighting a diverse bunch of sleepy babies.

Make Way for Cultural Exploration

As advocates of our culture, we ensure that the kids attend our cultural events, as most of the learning and interactions take place there. Similarly, trying to attend events that showcase the traits of other parts of the world is a great initiative. For instance, out of the many events and festivals that we attend, my daughter particularly loves the Chinese Lantern Festival. Apart from stunning and imaginative designs, these are great ways for our children to learn about the Chinese New Year celebrations and Asian cultures.

Try Visual Storytelling

"What is Day of the Dead or Día de Muertos", my daughter asked one day. She wondered if it was the Halloween of Mexico. I felt the best way of amplifying her awareness was to visually show her something age-appropriate and relevant. We watched the movie *COCO*, inspired by the Mexican 'Day of the Dead' holiday. The movie beautifully showcases the rituals and underlines on respecting ancestors; it also emphasizes on remembering the deceased loved ones for their contribution of eternal values; and teaches to celebrate life too. It made a forever imprint on her memory in a simple, yet enchanted way.

Children are adept at mimicking and learning just by observing. As it is said, *"Children are great imitators. So give them something great to imitate."*

Give Them Wings of Travel

As soon as my younger daughter turned one year old, we traveled to Turkey for our family vacation. Many will commiserate, for handling a toddler and a few months old baby together can be tricky at times. During the trip, my toddler kept asking questions, as she was observing varying traits of a country that enjoys a European, as well as an Asian aura. Food, language, architecture, attires, folklore, and anything that appeared different intrigued her. In one instance, she was fascinated by looking at the ancient ritual of the 'Whirling Dervishes' and wondered why people swirled rhythmically with their eyes closed. We told her that it's a deeply personal and intense form of meditation conducted to seek one with God. Although complex, we were able to teach her about the power of meditation too.

Remember, if you are tired, then you are doing it right. Pat on your backs!

Your parenting is perfect for your child and can never be faulty. It's important to remember that children will always learn at a pace and time agreeable to them.

So, whatever you do, do it with a flair of delight so that learning doesn't appear as a dreary task. After all, enjoyment is the prequel to the desire for knowledge!

It may seem like a 24x7 career, and the efforts may be endless, but let's face it! Seeing our children gradually shape as world changers with a global mindset will be extremely rewarding.

Regardless of how exhausting a day is, I always hug them with love and respect before saying goodnight. There is comfort and hope in my heart that tomorrow my children will also embrace diversity and humanity the same way.

ABOUT PURVI MANGTANI

With an MBA degree in Sales and Marketing and a prosperous corporate experience of 12 years, Purvi Mangtani (also known as Leena Asnanie) has a strong acumen for persuasive speaking and creative writing. Purvi is an Art and Travel Aficionado. She is currently exploring her affection for storytelling through photography and passion for mixed media through her new venture @cuesfromhues. Besides artworks, parenting, and content curation as a freelancer, she also enjoys writing her travel anecdotes on Instagram @milesupheart. She is a global citizen, currently based in Chicago, Illinois with her husband and two children. She believes that while it is imperative to adapt to changing times, one should never drift away from their aspirations.

Instagram: https://www.instagram.com/milesupheart/

Instagram: https://www.instagram.com/cuesfromhues/

Section IV
Language Learning

Chapter 25

Breaking the Barriers in Language Learning
Minali Bajaj-Syed

Conversation at a Coffee Shop in Florida...

Employee: Hi, what would you like to have today?

Me: A tall caramel macchiato please.

Employee: Will that be all?

Me: Yes please.

Employee: May I ask you something?

Me: Sure.

Employee: Do you by any chance speak Arabic?

Me (smiling): Yes, I speak a little Arabic!

Employee (happily): Really, no way!!

Marhaba! (Hello!) Kaifa Haluki? (How are you?)

Me: Anaa bi khair. (I am fine.) Wa inti? (And you?)

Employee (laughingly): Finally, someone who can speak to me in Arabic.

A short conversation in basic *Arabic* follows. She then goes on to upsize my coffee for free and provides excellent customer service.

So many of us who speak more than one language have had similar experiences, where speaking in one's own language or another language, has got us through some trouble or got us some freebies or simply made the opposite person friendlier towards us.

When I was studying in the US, I remember that if I ever needed to exchange an item at a store, I would ensure to first check and see which of the employees had a Hispanic name. I would then stand in that particular line and when I would get to the counter, I would start my conversation with *"Hola! Como estas?"*

Simply greeting someone or having a basic conversation in their language, can in the least warm up a stranger towards you. Makes me wonder - why is it that today's generation does not realize the value and importance of knowing more languages; and why have they found comfort and convenience in knowing just one language?

Growing up in Kuwait in the 80's, even before going to school, we learned multiple languages at home. We heard our parents speak in at least three languages – English (the global language), *Hindi* (the Indian local language) and our native language; and eventually we learned to speak them as well.

As kids, we perfected our English by watching Sesame Street and Disney Movies; learned new *Hindi* words from Bollywood movies; and picked up bits and pieces of *Arabic* by watching the famous *Arabic* cartoon *Captain Majid*.

The curiosity of learning new words and sentences from a different language was high!

When we traveled back to India during the summer holidays, we were loved and spoilt by our grandparents and the elders of our family. One of the reasons for this was because we could communicate with them in the native language and could relate to them. Most of them were not very well versed in English and spoke in *Hindi* or the native language.

I was one of the few grandchildren of the family, who knew how to speak *Sindhi* (my native language). I would love to sit with my paternal grandmother, who would speak to me in *Sindhi,* and I was always eager to reply to her in the same language. These rare moments, which at that time seemed insignificant, went on to actually teach me a new language. Then, I further got a chance to brush my new language skills, when I visited my maternal grandmother, who only spoke in the mother-tongue. All the other kids would communicate with her in broken words or with hand signs. No wonder, she always made me accompany her to the grocer and would get me little candies too (perks of communicating with her in a language she understood!)

Today, most young kids and youth do not find it necessary to know or learn their native or national language. Learning the local language seems like old-school to them. Even if their parents converse with them in the local language, they reply in English. **They seem to be lost in translation, while conversing with their grandparents or an elderly person, who does not speak English.**

The current generation has found comfort in one language and failed to realize the importance of being bilingual or multilingual. Speaking a new language is more challenging for the youth today than ever before, and there are many factors that contribute to this.

Barriers in the path of the new generation learning a new language include:

YouTube Generation

Almost all young kids and teenagers today have access to YouTube. Irrespective of the parental control settings, the language that dominates YouTube is English. These young minds are exposed to toy reviews, games, DIYs, cartoons, movies, etc. in one language; and eventually this language takes over the mind and they begin to process everything in a single language. For them, this is a norm and any other language sounds alien to them.

Social Media Norm

Instagram, Facebook, WhatsApp, and all other social media networking sites are in English. Changing language settings, posting something in the local language or replying in one's native language tends to make users feel that the person posting is from another generation or is not highly educated (read: profound in the English language!) We need to break away from this mindset and realize that knowing more than language is an asset and is greatly beneficial.

Parental Pressure

Some parents seem to be of the mindset that their children should master the English language to be successful in life. They ensure to talk in English at home and expect their children to speak in English at home and outside. If the child talks in the native language in front of others, the parents feel embarrassed. Most kids who grow up listening to their parents' converse only in English, learn just one language.

Shyness/Embarrassment

English seems like the norm to children whose parents do not encourage them to learn or speak their native or local language. Apart from English, all other languages sound foreign to them. Even if they understand what is being said in another language, they choose not to reply in the same language. Since it was never enforced upon them or they were not encouraged to speak in another language, they feel shy or embarrassed to speak in a second language, when they must. **Language learning is self-empowerment and not an embarrassment.**

Do we ever wonder why learning a new language is a feather in the cap?

Being bilingual or multilingual has many advantages and is always accompanied with a sense of pride. Knowing more than one language opens your dictionary and mind to a whole new world, literally!

In school, at the workplace, in the mall, at the airport, or in another country - it does not matter where you are. Speaking even a few words or sentences in another language and to be understood and comprehended, is a moment of joy and achievement.

Fortunately, today most schools and universities have made the learning of a second and/or third language compulsory. Even though my children already know two languages – English and *Hindi/Urdu*, they are also learning *Arabic* and *French*. The same goes with me. I speak English and *Hindi/Urdu*. I studied basic *Arabic* in school and beginner's *Spanish* at university. And currently, I am enrolled for a three-year *Arabic* program, to learn the language proficiently.

When my children visit their grandparents and communicate with them in their native language, I can see what a difference it makes to their relationship. It helps strengthen their bond, as well as it helps them relate to each other even better.

Whether it was a few decades ago or today, the power of being able to communicate in multiple languages is still extraordinarily strong. As responsible parents, we must motivate our children to learn multiple languages.

It is imperative that we make them realize how gratifying it is to know more than one language, and how it could help shape them into multilingual global citizens. As Frank Smith says, *"One language sets you in a corridor for life. Two languages open every door along the way."*

ABOUT MINALI BAJAJ-SYED

Minali Bajaj-Syed is the Managing Editor at RaisingWorldChildren.com.

She is an Indian, born and settled in Kuwait. Having lived in Kuwait, India, and the United States, she has had the wonderful opportunity to experience a diverse set of cultures.

Minali has a double degree in Arts and Education. Currently a homeschooling mom; she is a passionate mother of two kids. She is constantly learning, evolving, and trying to spread some positivity. Minali believes that being content and grateful to God is the key to happiness in life. She hopes to bring a change of heart and provoke the mind, through her writing.

Cooking scrumptious meals and baking desserts is an absolute stressbuster for Minali. She looks forward to sharing her quick and easy recipes with others around the world, through her Instagram handle 'Cinnamon_CardaMOM'

Instagram: https://instagram.com/cinnamon_cardamom

Website: https://raisingworldchildren.com/minali/

Chapter 26

Communicating Beyond Languages
Briana Marie

*"There was no language barrier when
it came to kids, and when it came to play."*
- Connie Sellecca

Diversity is certainly no stranger to our busy hometown. Our community is home to families from all walks of life, many of whom are planning for a short-term stay, after relocating for a job. Many of these families move several times during a calendar year. The children often struggle to make new friends and assimilate to a culture and language they are not familiar with.

I often remind my own children how such changes can be scary and difficult to deal with, in hopes that they can be both empathetic and understanding. *"What would you look for in a new friend, in a new place, where you can barely even speak the language?"*, I have asked my girls, and the answer is always the same.

It was the summer of 2018, when a new family moved in across the courtyard. My then 3 and 7-year-olds, watched as the movers loaded furniture into the once-vacant townhome across the lawn. *"Oooo...I hope they have kids!"*, my eldest daughter exclaimed, as she peeked through the blinds of our living room window. My children are always eager to make new friends, and it seems this neighborhood has a special way of attracting families with young children.

Hours went by, before we finally got to see the new family. My daughter had gotten her wish!

A family of five - mom, dad and three kids, who appeared to be between the ages of four and ten. We could not wait till they were settled in so we could go introduce ourselves.

A few days later, we saw three children come out to the courtyard to fly a kite, as their mom sat on the front porch and watched. My girls, who were sitting in front of our neighbors' house with a few other friends, decided to walk over and meet them. My eldest led the line of children eager to meet the new kids on the block. I watched from a distance as they proceeded to introduce themselves.

I could not hear the dialogue between the children, but I could see the look of confusion spread across each of their faces. Then slowly, my daughters and their friends turned away and began walking back, leaving the other three children to play with their giant airplane kite.

When the girls got closer, I asked them what had happened. All the children began to explain, one yelling over the other, that the new kids couldn't understand them. I chuckled and said, "Well, what exactly did you say?" They proceeded to explain that they were just greeting them with the typical "Hi, my name is . . ." However, when they asked if they wanted to play, things got a little confusing.

I smiled and said jokingly, "Well, I guess you have to find a language that you can all speak so that this will work huh?" Little did I know they would do just that!

Some time went by before my daughters attempted to interact with those children again. One day, when I was out toiling in my garden as the kids played in the courtyard, our new neighbors came to sit in the front yard. I figured it was a great opportunity to introduce myself and welcome them to the neighborhood. I remembered what the kids had told me about the language barrier, but I figured a smile and a handshake as I introduced myself would be sufficient.

My daughters followed behind me as I made my way across the yard. The woman stood up to greet me as I got closer. When I made it to her porch, I told her my name and explained that I lived across the courtyard. She smiled and told me her name. She then added, *"We just moved here from India. I am learning English still."*

I asked her what language she spoke, and she said *"Telugu."* I had never even heard of it, to be honest. I assured her that we are a remarkably diverse neighborhood, and that we all end up being like one big family despite our cultural differences.

I was so engrossed in the conversation with this sweet woman that I had not even noticed my kids playing in the field with 'the new kids on the block'. We both looked and smiled. "I see they made new friends!" I said. We watched as they worked together to assemble a new kite. There were lots of laughs as they struggled to get it exactly right. Everyone pitched in to try an idea they thought would work. After a few more minutes had gone by, they finally completed the project. Now, it was time to see if the kite would fly.

My daughters stood back, as the oldest boy began to run with the kite. All the children watched anxiously, as they knew getting the kite to fly would surely be a measurement of their success. Moments later, a beautiful multi-colored Octopus was flying high in the sky. The children were all so excited as they ran around the courtyard following the kite. Despite the language barrier, these new friends were able to successfully complete their kite-project. What seemed to be such a minor accomplishment, marked the beginning of a wonderful friendship between children who didn't even speak the same language.

We are still great friends with this family to this day. **We now understand that language is only a barrier if you allow it to** be. Something as simple as a smile can go a long way, and as the old saying goes, *"Actions speak louder than words."* We learn as we go and get creative in our communication efforts. This only adds more color to life and it is definitely something that I can appreciate.

Tips to overcome language barriers -

Smile

A simple smile can make others feel more comfortable, especially when in an unfamiliar environment. Even without speaking the same language, exchanging smiles can open the doors to a new friendship.

Keep it Simple

Use short sentences and simple words in your language. Many people understand phrases like, *"Hello, my name is..."* and *"Goodbye."*

Use Pictures

If you can't use your words to describe it, try drawing it out or finding a good picture online. Pictures can be great at depicting what words cannot explain. If you are welcoming a new neighbor, try making a card that shows two families standing in front of two different houses - one right next to the other - smiling and waving at one another. You can then add the word *"Welcome"* to the front of the car. This can also help teach a word in your language. It's a win-win!

Pointing Can Be Helpful

I know most of us have been taught that pointing is rude, but it can also be quite helpful in certain situations. You can point to objects as you speak, to help communicate your thoughts. It can also help those not familiar with the language to learn new words.

Rather than viewing linguistic differences as a barrier, look at it as an opportunity to learn more about yourself and the world around you. Yes, communicating when speaking different languages is a challenge, but it is one that can be successfully overcome. **Children can be some of the greatest teachers, and one thing we can learn from them is that using words is not the only way to communicate.**

"What would you look for in a new friend, in a new place, where you can barely even speak the language?" My daughters always give me an answer that I am sure many would agree with, ***"Kindness."***

ABOUT BRIANA MARIE

Briana Marie is a writer for Major League Mommy Blog, Posh Kids Magazine, and other media outlets. She is also a mother of two girls and founder of Tanzek Media - a Content Marketing and Digital Communications Agency based in the Midwest. Her extensive knowledge of global and digital communications has landed her features in numerous publications and podcasts including, Thrive Global and Authority Magazine.

Website: https://majorleaguemommy.com/

Instagram: https://www.instagram.com/majorleaguemommy/

Chapter 27

Using language to bond
Lup Wai

Mother tongue, is usually the language a person first hears and is first spoken from birth. Language is also a tool that allows us to express ourselves quickly and effectively, by externalizing our thoughts when we speak.

Language has become something that we take for granted. Being a Chinese living in a multicultural country, we have begun to speak more English than our own language. Furthermore, in schools, the main language is English, and our second language is Chinese. Hence, children growing up tend to speak more English than their own language.

I am a bilingual speaker and I speak English and Chinese. I was taught to speak the *Cantonese* and *Hakka* dialects by my parents and grandparents since I was young. *Cantonese* belongs to the Sino-Tibetan family of languages, developed from Middle Chinese. *"Canton"* refers to Guangzhou city, where the language first originated. Today, *Cantonese* is the third most widely spoken Chinese language worldwide.

Hakka is spoken natively by *Hakka* people throughout southern China, Taiwan, Hong Kong, Macau and in overseas Chinese communities around the world. It has many similarities with the *Gan* language, where both have borrowed many words from *Cantonese*.

While staying in Malaysia, we came across many people who spoke *Cantonese* and *Hakka*. We would speak in *Cantonese* very often, while in Kuala Lumpur. In different states of Malaysia, different languages were spoken.

No matter where we go, we tend to feel the closeness, whenever we speak in *Cantonese*; and we can feel the meaning of those words spoken in its original language.

As expected, being born in Singapore, the first language that my kids got acquainted with was English. As English is being used to communicate across different countries, we are slowly losing touch with our own native language. The younger generation speaks more English, and many don't even know what their native language is. As much as we want to communicate with a common language, we must also want to keep the native language as well.

One's native language is the language that creates a bond between people, as well as a sense of connectedness. When people have a common native language, there is a unique fondness and sharing of culture. Having someone speak the same language as you, increases friendliness and a sense of knowing the person.

I have taught my children the basics of *Cantonese* and they love it. While we travelled to Hong Kong for a short stay, they didn't feel excluded by the community as they spoke *Cantonese*. In fact, they felt secure and comfortable communicating. Although we are not their citizens, we were able to build the bond and reduce miscommunication and misunderstanding amongst us. The people in Hong Kong upon hearing us speaking *Cantonese* felt closer to us and were more inclined to help us when we needed assistance.

Our children saw the beauty of using language to bond and were very keen to learn a new language whenever possible. As parents, we always must be conscious and intentionally teach our children our native language or even a new language.

A new language may also be the one commonly used to communicate in the country you stay in. So, if you reside in such a country, then why not learn their language too?

Being able to guide our children allows them to create a strong link with the people, the language and the country. Having to learn and know each language encourages them to respect and love it.

I want to share how even sign language, is another language that greatly connects people together as well.

Once, we went to a Children's Foundation in Thailand. As we do not speak the Thai language, we had difficulty trying to tell people what we wanted. While the children gathered, I noticed everyone was just playing on their own. No one was communicating with each other, as there was no common language among them. I could see the barrier among them. But the moment the children started using sign language, they started to smile at each other and play together.

It is amazing how creative children are and how an unspoken language can create connectedness among them. It breaks the ice instantly!

Have you ever been stuck in a situation where no one understands your language and you cannot speak their language? What do you do?

You usually use your hand gestures to communicate right?

The world is a beautiful place and is filled with many beautiful cultures and languages. How awesome it will be to be able to learn all the languages. I really admire people who speak many languages on top of their native languages. Being multilingual, you get to connect with so many people from different places and religions and communicate with precision.

Honestly, just being bilingual has made our livelihood much easier when we travel abroad. Our children can communicate, study and play together without any difficulties.

Having the ability to speak the same language as others, and respecting their cultures allows us to feel included sooner. Inclusion is especially important when you are living abroad on your own.

The bond is instant when one knows how to speak a language that the other person understands. It bypasses race and social status. The deep bond of the language immediately bridges the gap, helps us break the linguistic barrier and brings us all together.

"Every new language we speak opens new possibilities" - Ali Anthony Bell

---

ABOUT LUP WAI

Founder of lupwaiparentwhisperer.com, Lup Wai is a Science educator and mother of 2 who shares her parenting and teaching experiences. Her interest in making learning fun and engaging has gained many parents' and educators' attention. She has been recognized in her local community as a path breaker and has collaborated with many educators to develop educational resources.

During her spare time, she loves to head out and explore nature, explore experiments with her children or catch up with friends.

Website: www.lupwaiparentwhisperer.com

Instagram: www.instagram.com/lupwaiparentwhisperer

Chapter 28

Effect of Language Learning on Growth
Shannon Lanzerotta

"If you talk to a man in a language he understands, that goes to his head. If you talk to him in his own language, that goes to his heart."
- Nelson Mandela

Embracing A Global Mindset Through Language

Did you know that teaching your child another language can actually raise his/her IQ?

Research has shown there are many benefits to being bilingual including:

- increased attention span

- better multi-tasking skills for older adults

- less cognitive decline

All of these benefits can be reaped by teaching your child one additional language, but what if your child (or you) know more than two languages? What additional benefits can be derived from multilingualism?

Currently, my son knows English, Italian and Spanish. He recently took an interest in Japanese because in 1st grade, his school offers a Japanese language immersion program. My son is in kindergarten, and his impatience at getting started on his fourth language is beginning to show. He has always been the only multilingual kid in the neighborhood. He takes great pride in his language knowledge.

Now, he sees his older friends learning a language he doesn't know, and he has been inspired to begin self-study by watching Japanese cartoons. I am intrigued by his competitiveness, and in a lot of ways I find it useful. How different would our world be, if kids competed in language development, similar to how they compete in sports?

My husband and I have talked with many of our neighbors about the Japanese program. My husband is happy to have our public school offer free language immersion, but many of our friends are not convinced. They do not see the usefulness of Japanese and wish the school would offer something more productive like Spanish or Mandarin. I understand that English, Spanish, and Mandarin are the top three most spoken languages in the world. I also know Japanese culture has many things to offer, and knowing the language is key to accessing all that amazing knowledge.

As a counselor, I see the acquisition of languages as reaching far beyond the obvious cognitive benefits. Don't get me wrong, I'm happy that we may have helped increase our son's intelligence but I'm more concerned about his overall life satisfaction. Studies tend to suggest that higher IQ ranges equal more happiness. Those with higher IQ tend to have higher paying, more stable jobs. They may also be better at identifying mental health issues and seeking help. I think it's more than that though, especially when it comes to multilingualism. I think the real benefit to being multilingual comes from an increase in EQ, not IQ.

Emotional intelligence (EQ) is, in my opinion, the key to real life satisfaction. Emotional intelligence is defined as the

ability to identify and manage one's own emotions, as well as the emotions of others. **What better way to understand someone, than to connect with them in their native language?** Language opens the door to cultural understanding.

It provides the opportunity to ask questions and gives multilinguistic exposure to other ways of being. The more languages your children know, the more opportunities they will have. They will have opportunities to build relationships with more people and they will have the opportunity to decide on what aspects of that language's culture resonates with them.

I think most parents will agree that teaching your child another language (or two) will benefit them in the long run. So why doesn't everyone do it? One of the most prevalent reasons I've heard is child resistance. Especially as children get older, it can become difficult to get them to embrace the completely foreign concept of another language.

My own son, who is now passionate about language, went through a resistant stage at 3 years old. Since he was born, his father spoke only Italian to him, and I spoke only English. When he was 6 months, I went back to work part-time and hired a Spanish nanny, who spoke exclusively Spanish. So, since he was a baby his world was multilingual. He did not know any other way, so that eliminated resistance. At 3, we moved away from his nanny, and he went for many months without Spanish exposure. Even though we kept up with Spanish cartoons, his fluency began to disappear. I knew that if I wanted him to keep his Spanish, I needed to hire help.

Upon introducing his new Spanish tutor, he refused to speak to her. He still retained some understanding, but his confidence in speaking the language was gone. He insisted she speak to him in English. She was exciting, fun, engaging and most importantly persistent. She never stopped speaking in Spanish and eventually, he gave in. He began learning the language again because he really liked her, and when you like someone, you want to connect with them. The relationship he began to develop with her became his motivation to learn her language. Language brings us closer. It is a beautiful thing if you think about it.

What can you do to inspire your child to embrace a new language? Here are three ideas that can get your child inspired:

Look into Local Programs

If you decide to send your child to preschool, see if there are any that offer bilingual curriculum. We started my son at a bilingual preschool around the same time we hired his Spanish tutor. They offered one hour of Spanish a day taught by a native speaker. It was a great way for my son to see his peers learning the language as well. For elementary school, check into local immersion or after-school programs. Also, you can look into local mom groups for meetups or classes.

Hire A Babysitter/Nanny from Another Country

One criterion we always had for childcare was that our son's caretaker speaks another language. We have hired wonderful people from all over the world, and it was the same price as hiring a monolingual (English) babysitter. Now that my son is older, we encourage them to talk about their country of origin and educate him about their culture. My son finds it interesting, and my husband and I get a weekly date night.

Ask Relatives to Speak in Languages They Know

We were also lucky to have Italian speakers in the family. Although they mostly speak English in their day-to-day life, we encourage them to speak Italian to our son. This is a great way for him to stay connected to Italy, the country of his ancestors. Many families have one or two bilingual/multilingual family members, who would be happy to share language with the children.

Remember, learning a new language is not just for kids.

You can reap the same benefits of multilingualism as your child. There are many great computer-based language programs available for adults. You could also hire a weekly language tutor for the whole family. Learning language and deepening cultural understanding is a great way to bring the entire family together and embrace the benefits of a global mindset.

ABOUT SHANNON LANZEROTTA

Shannon Lanzerotta is a licensed counselor with a Master of Science in Counseling and a Bachelor of Arts in Interpersonal Communication. She has worked in the behavioral health field since 2001, serving a variety of populations including children, families, couples and probationers. Shannon is certified in Equine-Assisted Psychotherapy, a therapeutic modality that uses horses to facilitate therapy sessions. She is also an educator and trainer of The Gottman Method, a research-based program for couples. Her passion is Holistic Behavioral Therapy™ which utilizes nutrition and mindfulness research to reduce anxiety, depression and many other mental health concerns.

Website: https://www.sistermom.com/

Chapter 29

The Impact of Emotions
Flor Garcia

It is 6 o'clock and the alarm just rang. It was time to get the kids ready for school. At the ages of 9, 8 and 7, anyone would think that getting ready to go to school is just a walk in the park. Not today. Not this week. Not this month. We just arrived in Germany and this is the first day in a German school and we don't speak a word of the local language.

Fear of failure rushes to my head. I feel my chest tighten, maybe an anxiety episode caused by our decision to send our three children to a local school, and not the international one recommended by everyone. I run to wake up my little ones, who are peacefully asleep. After a few kisses and warm hugs, they are up and running. They get dressed and sit down to have breakfast. I try to hide my emotions for I am afraid and I want to cry. Why am I doing this to my own kids? Will they hate me forever after today?

I drive them to school. They get out of the car, the three of them holding hands, and as they walk away from me towards the school entrance, I feel warm tears running down my cheeks. It is 7:15 am and my most precious treasures are about to experience the rough but very necessary awkwardness of walking into a place, without knowing how to communicate. And I am responsible for that!

"Believe in yourself! Have faith in your abilities! Without a humble but reasonable confidence in your own powers you cannot be successful or happy."

- Norman Vincent Peale

Did I just share this intricately emotional and personal moment? Yes I did, and I would do it again, if it helps you push yourself and your children outside of your comfort zone. This has been a very private moment that has existed every single day of our lives in Germany, as a reminder of the great achievements we are now able to accomplish.

Moving overseas and learning a foreign language, has been the most courageous act of love my husband and I have done for our kiddos. We wanted to provide them with the right tools to grow with a global mindset. Moving from the United States to Germany seemed to be the right step towards that goal.

But what about the feelings of our offspring? Did they want to move far away from their family and friends? The answer is both *Yes* and *No*. They were excited to see something new; but also extremely nervous about acquiring a new language and all the things this process implied:

- Finding new ways to communicate
- Working hard every day by learning vocabulary
- Grammar structures
- Making new friends
- Trying new foods
- Seeing distinct landscapes.

When to connect and provide emotional support to your child?

Dinner time was the moment to reinforce all the supportive feelings my husband and I were trying to provide our children with. It was the time to strengthen our bond with our kids, but many situations didn't go as smoothly as we expected. There were evenings filled with laughter as we joked about long indecipherable German words, or our strong Spanish accents. But we also hosted many dinners, where the main ingredients were tears from our children and us as well.

My oldest son felt pressured to perform well, since he thought we expected from him nothing less than straight A's. In the United States, he was at the top of his class; and moving to Germany placed him in a role he had never played before. Maybe, we failed at letting him know that his grades were not that important to us at that moment. What really mattered to us was his happiness and integration to the new culture. Once we talked to him about this issue, his mood was lighter, his tears less frequent and his smile bigger. As you may see, their language learning process was fully impacted by their emotions. Our approach as parents, in being sensitive to their emotions influenced the way our children acquired the German language.

When we think about school and specifically language courses, we tend to focus on intellectual skills, academics curriculums and concepts we want our children to learn. We frequently worry about the abilities of our kids to learn a second language and concentrate our efforts in providing the perfect academic opportunity to develop their language skills. But what about their motivation? What do we do with all the emotions related to learning something new?

Research suggests that students' emotions and motivations *(Affective Factors)* play an important role in the language learning process. It encourages us to pay close attention to how the learners feel about the target language and the course environment. Our child's motivations, attitudes and feelings influence the learning process, and we have to make sure to provide support for these emotional needs along the way.

176

"Motivation can be understood as a balancing act of the subjective value of the goal and the expectation that it can be achieved."
- Marilla D. Svinicki

These *Affective Factors* are the set of emotions and attitudes children have about themselves and their learning environment. We must embrace them as a reality in everyday activities, and as a powerful tool to promote success in acquiring a new language.

Alongside the tears and the fear of that first school morning in Germany, there were encouraging, supportive, cheerful, and hopeful words to offer emotional contentment to our kids. Our children were deeply impacted by our behavior and attitudes during those days; and they were ready to start this new chapter in their lives with a huge smile and gigantic motivations. They knew it would not be easy, but they were conscious about the value of learning a new language and experiencing a distinct culture.

Once we realize that inhibitions, self-esteem, attitudes, and anxiety play a decisive role in language learning, we can come up with a plan to make language learning the most rewarding journey ever. Consequently, it is important to pay close attention to our child's developmental stage, to craft the best strategy of emotional support during this exciting but challenging time, without disrupting their cognitive and psychological growth.

Here I bring some of my family's tips for a happy language learning experience. Please use them as guidelines to create your own.

I frequently have to remind myself, as should you that every family is unique, and advice needs to be moderated to fit its individuality.

Your Expectations Are Not Your Child's Reality

Usually, our expectations become strict objectives to be achieved to be successful, causing us stress and anxiety. Therefore, it is important as parents to adjust our levels of assumptions and beliefs high enough to empower our children, but low enough to avoid putting an extra load of expectations on top of their shoulders. We recommend establishing clear goals and milestones, previously discussed as a family, to guarantee that our expectations match our children's.

Share Your Own Fears to Normalize Feelings of Inadequacy

One thing I have seen, during my years as a language educator and mother of three multilingual children, is the feeling of inadequacy experienced by learners when acquiring a foreign language.

I felt it myself as well, both when I learnt English and German. We often think that the language is too difficult to learn or that we have a strong accent that makes us sound ridiculous. What can we do? I purposely share my own fears and emotions with my kiddos. I explain to them that it is normal to be afraid of something unknown and that many times I question my own abilities to achieve a goal too.

Normalizing these filters of your own, would empower your children with the required tools to better handle difficult situations, while recognizing their own feelings. When my children feel inadequate to continue learning the German language or starting with a new one (we all want to learn French), we sit down together and talk about our fears. Then we focus on all those strengths we have shown in other challenging situations and how victorious we came out of them. Sometimes we just need to be reminded, humbly, of how awesome we are. A relaxed atmosphere is key!

Planning a movie night at home on Saturday, visiting a local ethnic supermarket, or watching some online videos in the target language are fun and effective ways to support language learning at home, in a more relaxed environment. After the pressure of language courses and school, our little ones would benefit from some quality time exposed to the target language, without the demands to perform in front of a stranger.

Be Mindful of Criticism

Time together can also help you keep track of different levels of fluency and accomplished milestones. Just remember, this is a moment to ease up on your child and observe them. Do not criticize his or her language skills. If I see the need to correct grammar mistakes or pronunciation, I usually do it by raising my eyebrows and repeating what my child has said, but in a corrected form. Don't overdo it though! You want to favor fluency and emotional health, not pure accuracy.

Our child's success highly depends on the support and motivation we provide them for achieved goals and dreams. Let's continue exciting our children about their goals and ambitions. Show that you are excited for them too. Your positive energy and adrenaline will push them to continue their hard work and be happy with their efforts. **Learning a new language can be a daunting task, but the right emotional support and attitude could be an open door towards globally minded children and future leaders of the world!**

ABOUT Flor Bretón-García

Flor Bretón-García is a Venezuelan lawyer and linguistics specialist, who has transited expat life since 2002. She currently lives in Germany, where she works as a language and intercultural consultant. Flor shares her passion for her mother tongue, Spanish, by teaching online and in-person. She is also an advocate for expat women empowerment, especially those who move overseas in a less privileged position. Flor began her journey as a social entrepreneur with her project Little Nómadas in 2016 and since then she has assisted many Latino families moving overseas.

Website: https://littlenomadas.com

Instagram: https://www.instagram.com/littlenomadas/

Section V
Celebrating Diversity

Chapter 30

Teaching Kids About New Festivals
Briana Marie

"The greatness of a culture can be found in its festivals. "
- Siddharth Katragadda

American, Japanese, Indian, Russian, Korean, and Mexican: our community is filled with families from different backgrounds. We are blessed to live in a truly diverse community: a community that genuinely welcomes diversity. We are able to learn so much about the world without ever having to leave our tiny little community. We get to try foods from different cultures, learn about different religious practices, and learn about special celebrations that take place in other countries. It can be a lot for my children to take in, but we have found that one of the best ways to learn about these other cultures is through their festivals.

The diversity in our community allows us to have access to a wide variety of cultural festivals, and I make it a priority to attend as many as my schedule allows. However, I find that many others in my community exclude themselves from some of these festivals, as they feel that it is organized only for a select group of people. They don't want to feel as if they are appropriating other cultures, by attending a festival dedicated to a particular region or background.

I view this idea differently.

Attending a festival that is not typical of your culture gives you an opportunity to learn more about the world around you. It is a way to become more accepting of those from other backgrounds.

It is an opportunity to step outside of your comfort zone, and view life from a new lens. These festivals aren't meant to exclude, they are organized in the spirit of community.

I feel that it is important to teach our children early to embrace other cultures and lifestyle differences. When I attended the India Day Festival in our hometown, I found that I was able to learn so much about the country and its people. We have an exceptionally large Indian population where we live, and I figured attending one of their largest festivals in our town was one of the best ways to familiarize ourselves with their culture. My children had lots of questions during our attendance, and what better place to ask those questions than in the vicinity of thousands of individuals who would have the answer!

After the festival, we talked about the different foods we tried, the new things we learned, and what we enjoyed most. My daughters couldn't wait until the next large cultural event came to town. So, when October 31 came around that year, in addition to our normal Halloween fun, we attended a *Dia de los Muertos* festival. *Dia de los Muertos* is a Mexican holiday that we were familiar with by name, but not by practice.

We learned that *Dia de los Muertos* is not about celebrating death. It is about reuniting the living and the dead. During this celebration, families create altars or offerings which include marigolds for their deceased family members. This is their way of encouraging visits from the departed and inviting them to the celebration. We all found this concept quite interesting, and it said a lot about the Mexican culture and their beliefs. We tend to view death as a somber event, whereas in this culture death was celebrated and honored as a part of life. As we decorated and devoured sugar skull cubes, we got to enjoy a discussion about the spiritual meaning behind the items used in the offering. We also discussed the differences between the *Dia de los Muertos* celebration and our traditional Halloween celebration, which takes place on the same day. It was yet another educational moment, to say the least.

When we are not attending local festivals, we are still finding creative ways to learn about different celebrations from other parts of the world. From Youtube, to checking out books in the library, we can continue our learning about festivals across the globe.

Without spending tons of money on traveling, our children can get a good feel of the world by attending new festivals. They will understand how to respectfully interact with those from different backgrounds, and ultimately learn we are not so different from one another after all.

Ways to teach kids about new festivals -

Visit Local Festivals

Take advantage of the festivals your city has to offer. Contact your city's parks and recreation services department to find out what cultural festivals they may have in the works. Joining in on the action is one of the best ways to learn about the celebration. It also makes for a cool and educational, family outing.

Keep a Calendar of Holidays

Consider purchasing a global calendar that includes holidays from all over the world.

This is a great way to keep up with the different celebrations taking place throughout the year. Once you have an awareness of what celebrations are taking place on any given day, you can join in the celebration by taking the time to learn more about specific festivals taking place in honor of that special day.

Use the Internet to Learn

The internet gives us access to a great deal of information. From a quick Google Search, to an explanatory YouTube video, you can be sure that you will find more information on the different festivals being celebrated across the globe.

Read Books Together

There is nothing like good old-fashioned learning. Check out a few books relevant to the festival you would like to learn about at your local library. You can read these books as a family and share your thoughts on your newfound knowledge. This is not only a great learning opportunity but a fantastic opportunity to bond as a family as well.

When it comes to teaching kids about new festivals, there is certainly no single correct way to go about doing so.

It does not have to be made a chore; it should instead be a fun family activity. Through the act of learning about different festivals, children not only learn about the world. . . they learn acceptance.

ABOUT BRIANA MARIE

Briana Marie is a writer for Major League Mommy Blog, Posh Kids Magazine, and other media outlets. She is also a mother of two girls and founder of Tanzek Media - a Content Marketing and Digital Communications Agency based in the Midwest. Her extensive knowledge of global and digital communications has landed her features in numerous publications and podcasts including, Thrive Global and Authority Magazine.

Website - https://majorleaguemommy.com/

Instagram - https://www.instagram.com/majorleaguemommy/

Chapter 31

Making Festivals Relatable Today
Lup Wai

*"Finding common ground among faiths can help us
bridge needless divides, at a time when unified
action is more crucial than ever."*
- Dalai Lama

Do you celebrate festivals like your parents used to?

There are many different types of festivals celebrated around the world. The purpose of any celebration is to create a strong bonding with the people around you, who share the same culture as you. Celebration of festivals also allows us to take a break from what we usually do and step away from the stress of work, by spending time with our loved ones. It is a way to create memories of important occasions.

Though there are many different types of festivals being celebrated in different countries, the main goal of these celebrations is the same - to rejoice togetherness and life. One may even meet people, who have the same interest as you, thus creating new friendships from there.

As the world changes, traditional festivals have also evolved and are not limited to their core cause. Together, with modernization and commercialization, ways of commemoration are being modified as time goes by.

How about cultural celebrations? Which cultural celebrations do you celebrate every year?

There are many traditional festivals still being carried out in many different countries because of their impact and integration to our environment and livelihood.

Traditional festivals such as Chinese New Year, Christmas, *Diwali* have extraordinarily rich cultural backgrounds, hence they can attract attention worldwide and people from all over the world participate in it.

Advent of Technology & Business into Life

Most festivals involve delicious authentic delicacies. Traditionally, when the festival was around, our mothers and grandmothers would spend a lot of their time making all these yummy goodies for the family, relatives and friends.

Now, as most modern mothers are working, they do not have the luxury of time to make these goodies. Instead, they purchase these delicacies from others who make them. Hence, commercial businesses grab this chance to produce these products; and at the same time modernize it to attract more consumers.

Other traditional ways of celebrating, such as by using candles, are now being replaced with lights to avoid fire hazards. Traditional costumes are being replaced with modern clothing. The yearly affair of shopping together as a family, to get all that is needed for the festivals, is being replaced with the convenience of online shopping.

The mix of the new way and traditional ways of celebration has unknowingly created an insightful blend of contemporary and customary update of the tradition.

Celebrate Traditions through a Different Country's Culture

It can be overwhelming and exciting at the same time when living in a different country and having to learn another culture, while still staying connected and grounded to our own culture.

Looking at it through a different perspective, we get to explore and adapt to the celebration of the local holidays and traditions of the new country. We can even infuse fun and creativity into different cultural celebrations.

Let's think out of the box on how to celebrate the traditional festivals with a twist. For example, during Christmas, instead of having the usual turkey and ham, we can eat cultural themed food such as *Mithai* (sweets) from India, *Kebab* from Turkey, or *Paella* from Spain. We may also take the chance to teach family and children how to greet or say well wishes in another language.

Nurturing New Relationships

For our traditional holidays, we should invite friends, neighbors and colleagues' home for a celebration. Having new friends from all walks of life, joining us during our celebrations will allow us to connect with them. It will help us create new friendships, as well as opportunities for our children to learn more about their cultures.

If you are worried that your new friends may not adapt to your traditional foods, then make your get-together a potluck style. In this way, everyone gets to bring their own food according to their own palette and diet. Besides, you get to have a variety of food to serve your guests too!

Great memories are created, when we observe our traditions with new friends in another country. Why is this so? It is because we get drawn into a preparation and celebration mode, and invite all our new friends to join us. In addition, it contributes to a sense of comfort and belongingness, while establishing connections between different generations that brings everyone together.

During this time, everyone gets to know each other better by exchanging tidbits of their life in a new place. It also makes one feel grateful for having each other's company. This allows everyone to foster respect and open-mindedness for other cultures.

So, the next time you see that your traditional holiday is approaching on the calendar, do not forget to start planning early, invite your friends and create your own lasting memories!

ABOUT LUP WAI

Founder of lupwaiparentwhisperer.com, Lup Wai is a Science educator and a mother of 2 who shares her parenting and teaching experiences. Her interest in making learning fun and engaging has gained many parents' and educators' attention. She has been recognized in her local community as a path breaker and has collaborated with many educators to develop educational resources. During her spare time, she loves to head out and explore nature, explore experiments with her children or catch up with friends.

Website: https://lupwaiparentwhisperer.com/

Instagram: https://instagram.com/lupwaiparentwhisperer

Chapter 32

Incorporating Cultures into Celebrations
Johana Castillo

*"Each culture is a system of values which may
well complement the values in another."*
- Ruth Benedict

We all started as being naturally curious children. Our continual mission was to learn, to discover and to feel awe with everything that happened during our day. I remember always being on the move: checking everything, how my family did things, what we celebrated, what we ate, how we danced. I deeply enjoyed those celebrations that involved our family getting together in the same place, with many new faces, food, music, familiar and unfamiliar. For me, the games and freedom of playing with my sister, cousins, neighbors, and friends during a celebration, are one of the most fantastic memories I have from my childhood.

And here I am, still eternally curious. I love to learn from others and from our environment, including animals and nature. When I grew up, I realized that as a child my mother had a hard time with me because I am fairly sure I have ADHD. That active curiosity has always helped me make friends, reach out to others, and try new things. There is no surprise that my passion has always been people!

Learning about others and their customs, their traditions, their feelings, and their history makes me feel deeply connected to them in many ways. I have always thought that if I learn more about other humans, I can understand a little bit more about myself.

I was born in Bogotá, Colombia, and came to live with my mother in the United States when I was 16 years old. Here, I met my partner who is from Honduras, and after five years of our relationship, we decided to start a home. Later, we decided to raise children, and now, we have two global citizens in training!

When we started raising children, we felt a huge need of teaching them about our culture, traditions and celebrations that had a meaning for us as a family. When you are an immigrant, many times you are questioned about your identity, values, culture. All these pesky interrogations are common to parents raising children outside of their native countries.

We consciously tried to become aware of the value of our culture, traditions, and community, in the places we liked to call home. We agreed to raise children who would hold a strong sense of themselves and have a compassionate global point of view. We were disappointed to find the need for people to put labels and have expectations of us, based on stereotypes. We know that the only way to really get to know a person, is to get to know them, as friends!

One of the many values that we have always wanted to infuse in our home is the awareness that our cultures are not the only ones that exist in the world. We understand that we can learn and support others: by upholding knowledge about the different cultures that exist in our local community, and by upholding and caring for them just as equals.

If you decide to start incorporating other cultures in your traditions and festivities, here are some useful and concrete steps that will help you to achieve it:

192

Personal Awareness

When we come to celebrate cultural traditions, our family has prioritized those celebrations that hold a personal connection to our lives and heritage or bring deep and meaningful value to us as a family. Personally, I refuse to celebrate offensive celebrations like Columbus Day. I think about the historical value and connection with the values that I am modeling at my home; and acknowledgment and respect about other cultures must be included.

Some people love different cultural celebrations but do not acknowledge or show respect to the people of that culture. Any lack of respect and knowledge, for the groups of people that historically celebrated or originated these festivities, can cause terrible damage to our multicultural relationships. It can be a source of disconnection and dehumanizing others. Celebrating cultural events should always come with deep respect and acknowledgement for the group of people that uphold this celebration.

For example, *Cinco de Mayo*. Many people in the United States think that is the day of Independence of Mexico. The focus of that day is mainly Margaritas and Tacos. Sadly, the decorations and even the advertisement is highly stereotypical, showing persons with big sombreros and mustaches. If we inquire a little about this celebration, we can learn that *Cinco de Mayo* is about Mexican pride over a military victory against a French Batallion in 1862, but it is not one of their main national celebrations. On the *Cinco de Mayo* celebration in the United States, the total disregard of the original culture and community we see it as a total disgrace. Sadly, as a culture, we witness that some people that enjoy the culture, food and music from Mexico, are very disrespectful of Mexicans or people with Mexican descent.

It is not that difficult currently, to find reputable sources of knowledge, which can educate us on ways to observe celebrations and traditions correctly; as well as learn about different ways of supporting these people. Imagine, having cultural knowledge and practical ways to support others: that would make for a great real learning experience!

When we teach our children about cultural celebrations, teaching them about the origins of that tradition and our connections with a celebration by using our personal stories, can be an excellent first step. Using our childhood memories, or stories of how a specific culture is important or relevant to our family can be so much fun and support their sense of identity!

For our family and I, this special celebration is *'El Día de la Velitas'*. I grew up celebrating this day every year on December seventh. *Día de las Velitas* is a celebration that comes from the Catholic syncretism with original beliefs in Colombia and was established in 1854. It talks about bringing light to the world, and it is celebrated in honor of the image of the Virgin Mary, the sacred femenine that portrays many of the intricate beliefs of many faiths around the world.

Awareness of Other Cultures

When we choose cultural or traditional events, it can be highly educational, if we offer the history or background about the celebration. This can be particularly useful in creating a rich family culture and a reflective spirit.

For *'Día de las Velitas'* traditionally, families and friends create or buy paper lanterns that are positioned in front of their houses. I remember the beautiful and resourceful decorations that we created every year, and above all, I remember the sense of community. When we decided to make *'Día de las Velitas'* one of the main celebrations at our home, we created an atmosphere, where all our friends and neighbors felt comfortable coming to our house that day and being part of it.

We craft paper lanterns with the children. That always doubles as an art and craft project. I usually have a table ready with simple templates, paper, stickers, paints and little tea candles for this purpose. Some years we make them round, other times we make them square. It varies as per the age of the children and their abilities. But everyone, adults and children, are encouraged to create.

The concept of bringing light to the world is a universally correlated concept with many other faiths and beliefs around the world. The *Hindu* religion has its Festival of Lights, *Diwali*. *Judaism* also has a commemoration of their miracle of lights, Chanukah. In the Islamic faith, the guidance from God is referred to as light.

Recognizing everyone's value in our celebration is the highlight of our *Dia de las Velitas*. I encourage the conversation to talk about the contrast and similarities between our stories, lives, and traditions. That is what creates conscious global citizens!

In this celebration, I had been conscious of offering cultural aspects that do not represent a single faith or a belief but all the facets of the infinite universe of all our personal experiences. The single act of getting together as a community and sharing time across generations is most precious. Seniors enjoy the company of the children and vice-versa. Adults interact with children of all ages. Children observe adults and other children. Celebrations are great places to learn!

Food

We invite all our guests to bring a dish, dessert, or drink that reminds them of this particular time of the year; in our case, it comes in December for *Día de las Velitas*. Our table is full of delicious foods that are varied to the taste and needs of everyone.

I usually ask if there are any special dietary needs or allergies, and I have tried to create vegan alternatives to the traditional

Colombian dishes that I prepare for this occasion. I am always so happy to see everyone, from children to adults, share their history behind a dish's recipe or ingredients, while some are trying many things for the first time. Like the time when my friends tried *Pozole* (Mexican Hominy Soup), or when we bring varied selections of the same dish but from different countries, like the *Empanadas* (corn or flour dough with varied fillings). In Colombia, traditionally in December, we share *Natilla* (Colombian corn custard) and *Buñuelos* (fried cheesy balls). But the table is also full or tamales, tortillas, different types of pastas, soups and desserts that reflect all of the people in our community!

Music

Throughout the night, we ask the guests to contribute to the playlist with their own music. Learning about everyone's favorite songs creates a diverse listening environment. When we play music in different languages, we encourage language learning and environments, where many languages are represented.

We enjoy our *Cumbia* (AfroLatin music) rhythms, as well as our Greek dances (*Sirtaki, Kalamatianos*), Arab music, any other type of traditional end of the year songs and many more that can reflect the diversity of our community roots. I have learned firsthand from many the proper way to dance certain songs, the story behind a genre or dance and personal stories tied to style of music. Music is marvelous! And supports the universal language of love and fun, bringing us together through its infinite rhythms! We can share so much through this language!

If you are looking for variety, many online radios have World Music stations. Also, remember to have an accessible area to double as a dance floor space. A little research beforehand can make a big difference. Also, if you can have live music, encourage all your guests to bring their favorite instruments and join the fun! Many cultures enjoy dancing, as music is an essential element for any cultural celebration.

Intergenerational and Intercultural Spaces

As I mentioned before, it is imperative to remember that our celebrations have the potential to share knowledge from one generation to another; and to share opinions and ideas of different cultures in a familiar and friendly space. Working towards creating these spaces is part of the care we put into planning it.

Ensuring to offer spaces for babies (diaper changing spaces) and children (free play and safe), for seniors (easy access and comfortable), and for people with different physical needs (inviting and accessible) is a question of inclusion. At the same time, offering a safe space without judgment or long interrogations between friends (different genders), can be so refreshing.

I also want to mention the need for consent. Consent must be shared on all parties regardless of their age, genre, sexual orientation or cultural background. Expressions such as kisses, hugs, even dancing may not have the same context for others, that is why it is always wonderful to ask first. As we understand that other cultures may have different ways to see, behave and interact that are culturally acceptable for them, consent needs to be explicit and always present in these spaces. This is a key part of what we named as creating safe spaces to be who we are and to grow and interact.

We can hope that all these celebrations include a positive attitude, where racist or stereotypical comments will not be tolerated. Many times, comments about a dish or the way someone looks or talks, can be contrasted with education and a short explanation. I usually have to explain to the children about the ingredients of a dish, about the flavors or how many familiar ingredients can be used to make a variety of dishes.

Creating these spaces can many times prove to be difficult. Reaching out to your friends for help, trying to figure out, and asking them, having these conversations, and including others in our planning are great ways to solve this problem. They can choose to elaborate on the topic or not, that is alright! Remember, it is also about finding a safe and sacred space between humans.

About actual spaces to celebrate our event - if we do not have a home that can offer accessible spaces, perhaps we can use a community center, a faith space, a natural area or a cultural place to elope and celebrate. In the past, we have made a ramp at the entrance of our house for persons with a wheelchair. The mere fact that we acknowledge everyone is needs, reflects the love and care we have for our community!

Also, we try to provide opportunities to everyone, which gives them a chance to share their personal knowledge. For *Día de las Velitas*, we create our own paper lanterns; similarly, children and adults can create their own version. I still remember the year when my Swiss friend created her own lantern with a turnip! Our Mexican friend shared that they did the same in different parts of Mexico. We rejoiced in finding commonalities in all our ways of celebrating. These little interactions go a long way.

Since the beginning of this tradition, I started reserving a time in the evening, where everyone in the room who felt comfortable, would answer a question or tell us a story on how they celebrated that time of the year in their households. One year I asked, *"What is the food that gives you the most memories of December?"* The answers were a beautiful reflection of childhood memories: sometimes sad, sometimes happy, many melancholic; some reflecting on little details of how their mother would make a special dish just for that time of the year; or how the weather, social or economic situations, affected their circumstances at that time of the year. We also invite all the children to listen and to share. Remembering that in this exchange, we find humanity in others and we learn about them. Usually, the children love this exercise!

Some other stories would give us an insight of another country or culture full of traditions. Having time to have the adults and children sharing their personal stories is so beautiful! All our stories are worthy of mention, and when we have the opportunity to say them aloud, it can be very healing. The most exciting part of trying to take into consideration all the different cultures in our celebrations is that every year, we are supporting community and new memories.

This type of learning is a crucial part of a culturally aware home and in raising successful world citizens. Our world is rapidly changing. Now the views of a virus and many other situations that make gatherings harder, are indeed making us thankful for the times we were able to be with others and celebrate. I say, let us find new, different ways to do this. Feel encouraged to offer these spaces wherever you go. Know the goodness that can come out of those meetings, or offer safe spaces for members in your community, we need this more than ever! We can create these spaces with our mere presence in a public space, at work, school, or any circles we are part of. Incorporating organic and effortless ways, to learn about others and their cultures, is easier if we:

- Try to create and sustain close and meaningful friendships with people from many different backgrounds and cultures.

- Cook and taste different types of food on a regular basis.

- Listen, create, dance, and enjoy an ample variety of music.

- Offer your gifts to your community! You will always be needed.

- Read and buy a varied selection of printed materials and books that reflect the many cultures. Choose to buy and read own voices over the narratives that are from the outsider perspectives.

- Celebrate traditional celebrations from our own cultures, as well as accompany others to celebrate theirs with respect.

- Believe and support multilingualism (language learning) at every level of education and society.

- Acknowledge others and their cultures the same way you acknowledge yours.

- Take time to learn about the origins of different celebrations as well as the celebrations you chose to celebrate as a family.

- Be mindful on how your culture and celebrations can be perceived by others. Centering your own celebrations and culture, will not leave space for others to share theirs with you.

- Support others from the heart to create spaces that are safe for you and for ALL!

Our world can be profoundly transformed if we create friendships to teach our children the beauty of every culture. Our lives can be changed and improved by really getting to know others and their families. We all have some time to offer and to learn from each other, let us start doing it in the middle of a celebration!

ABOUT JOHANNA CASTILLO

Johana was born and raised in Colombia and is the founder of Mama Tortuga.org - a multicultural, mindful bilingual website for parents who want to raise global citizens. She is a lover of nature, culture, and languages; is a backyard gardener; and has a background of anthropology and nursing studies. She has served as a parent advocate in her local school board and now is homeschooling her two children, she has been featured on several global publications and websites. She believes that our mission as parents and educators is to empower others to offer their unique gifts for the common good of all in their community. She offers classes, speaks at conferences and organizes events that bring awareness to our multicultural connections and relationships. She is the organizer of Moon Talk for Teenage Girls and Moon Talks for Women classes in West Palm Beach FL.

Website: www.mamatortuga.org

Instagram: https://www.instagram.com/mamatortuga/

Chapter 33

Instill Diversity Through Food
Nupur Biswal

Why is it important for children to try foods from other parts of the world?

When my elder daughter first started kindergarten, I used to pack her favorite Indian meals like *idli*, *dosa*, *chapati*, *puri* or rice in her lunch box. Few months into school, she became hesitant to take Indian foods in her lunch box. She kept arguing with me about why I couldn't give her normal food like others. I tried to explain to her that our food is also 'normal', but she was too adamant.

Day by day the conditions became worse, and some days she used to buy food from the cafeteria to eat. It was not that she didn't like Indian food anymore; she was eating the same food happily at home. It was just that other children in her class had never tried or seen Indian foods before. So, for them Indian foods were strange and, in their words, *"Not Normal!"*

They used to tease my daughter, sometimes bully her, or curiously ask her tons of questions about the food. She eventually got tired of it and was reluctant to have any more Indian food in her lunch box.

So I talked to the members of PTO at her school, and planned a Global Lunch at her school during the Thanksgiving Party. We requested each child in her class to bring one item from their own cuisine or their favorite cuisine for the potluck. And guess what, we all had a blast at the party trying out so many new and different varieties of food items, from different parts of the world. All the children were happy to learn about the unusual looking foods and stopped criticizing the *"not so normal foods"*.

In my opinion, children should learn to celebrate differences and appreciate things that make others (and themselves) unique. This helps them with their own self-esteem and teaches them to attribute value to every person, no matter how different or similar they may be. Children need to be shown that *"different"* does not mean *"strange," "weird,"* or *"wrong"*. It is as normal as theirs!

Another benefit of introducing children to a variety of cuisines at an early age: it will help them explore a variety of tastes from other parts of the world, and it will enhance their food palate as well.

What are some lessons that can be learned from global foods?

Here are few activities and ideas that can be helpful in cultural introduction for children through various cuisines. These activities can be done in schools, libraries or in a multicultural community or at home, if you have a bunch of diverse friends.

Friendship Snack Mix

Ask each child to bring about a half cup of their favorite snack like cereal, raisins, crackers, etc. When you get all of the snacks: mix them all in a huge bowl and serve it as one snack.

Talk about how different things go together to make something incredibly good and much more flavorful. This helps understand the idea of diversity: how people from diverse backgrounds can make our lives more interesting.

Apples – Different Colors but All the Same Inside

Set a red, yellow and green apple on a table. Then ask the children to name the colors.

Peel the apples and talk about how they have different colors on the outside but are the same on the inside, just like people. Discuss how people are different by their appearance on the outside, but on the inside, we are all the same! From this activity they will learn to treat all colors of people equal.

This activity can be done with different colors of eggs as well.

Arrange Global Dinners

This activity can be done at home or in school. We enjoy global dinners at our home, not just because of the various yummy foods, but also because we learn about the different place/country that the food belongs to. On weekends, we like to watch various YouTube videos and try to learn how to prepare different cuisines; and then do the grocery shopping together; and also discuss how similar or different the ingredients are from ours.

Here are a few things that we learned from different cuisines around the world.

Thai Cuisine

Thai cuisine is heavily influenced by ancient traditions and influenced by Vietnamese and Chinese cuisines too. Thai chefs rely on aromatic, savory dishes with a gorgeous presentation. If you can nail the presentation, great! If not, just have fun with it.

Set the table with a length of Thai inspired elephant-print fabric. Pick up Thai take-out or even grab something from the freezer section of your supermarket. If your child is older, let him/her help you make a *Pad Thai* meal. As you dine, let your child roll lettuce wraps of rice and the savory Thai meats.

Over the dinner share some fun facts about Thailand:

- Siamese Cats are native to Thailand, not China.
- The Thai language is an offshoot of Chinese.
- *Buddhism* is Thailand's largest religion.

Indian Cuisine

The cuisine of India is one of the world's most diverse cuisines, characterized by its sophisticated and subtle use of many spices, vegetables, grains and fruits grown across India. India's religious beliefs and culture have played an influential role in the evolution of its cuisine. Vegetarianism is widely practiced in many *Hindu*, *Buddhist* and *Jain* communities.

Decorate the table with pieces from India like elephants, lamps, *diyas* (traditional candles) or just with simple colored paper. Greet everyone in *Hindi* saying *"Namaste!"* Play some Bollywood music in the background, and post dinner everyone can dance to it and have some fun.

Try to prepare authentic Butter Chicken and pair it with some *Naan* (Indian bread), which is easily available at any grocery store.

Children would definitely love some Mango *Lassi* (Indian milkshake)!

Share some fun facts about India:

- The *Taj Mahal* (a famous mausoleum) is one of the seven wonders of the world, and is located in *Agra*, a northern town of India.
- *Varanasi* - One of the oldest inhabited places in the world; this holy city is at least 3000 years old.
- India has the second largest population in the world, with over 1.2 billion people.

Italian Cuisine

Who does not love Italian food? To most children, Italian cuisine is synonymous with pizza. Let's expand their horizons!

Kids love to eat with their hands, so make easy *antipasti* for dinner. Pile a platter with plump and colorful olives, hard cheese such as *Pecorino*, and Italian cured meats. Serve crusty Italian bread dipped in olive oil with herbs. Enjoy a meal of heavy appetizers.

Share these fun facts about Italian culture:

- The primary religion in Italy is Catholic.
- Some of the greatest artists in history were Italian.
- The national music of Italy is *Opera*.

Mexican Cuisine

If you have a world map, point out where Mexico is; talk about their native language; discuss how Mexico has influenced our culture through food and music.

Decorate the table with bright colors and pick up a pair of *maracas* from the party store. It's time for a fiesta!

Seriously, this is a great teaching opportunity. Your children probably already love Mexican food, so make homemade cheese *quesadillas* and *guacamole* and learn about Mexico.

Here are a few facts about Mexico to share with your child:

- The jungles of Mexico are home to parrots, jaguars, and iguanas. It's a bio-diverse rainforest.
- The *Aztec* (natives) of Mexico invented Hot Chocolate.
- *Mariachi* is the nation's favorite music.

Some points to remember:

- If you can't or don't want to prepare all these foods by yourself, then just try to order it from a restaurant.

- Turn off the television during this special dinner.
- Remain positive! Even if they don't like to try the food, discuss facts about the cultures and take it as a learning opportunity.
- Have a tablet handy to explore images of artwork or listen to music from that culture.
- Make this a special occasion, maybe once a week or two: depending on your child's age and attention span.
- When including others from your community or school in your meals, be very aware of allergies. It is a bit of extra work, but totally worth making each kid feel included.

These are just a few examples, but the possibilities to teach about culture through international cuisine are vast. With some imagination and effort, you can transfer your family and guests to any part of the world and teach something that will stay with them lifelong.

International cuisines are diverse, colorful, and amazing. Children, especially younger ones, are open-minded to new ideas. **Take advantage of their natural curiosity and expand their horizon in any possible manner.**

ABOUT NUPUR BISWAL

Nupur Biswal is an ex-software engineer turned STEM educator & Marketing and Social Content Creator for multiple companies. She lives in San Antonio Texas, with her husband and two children. She is an active member of PTO of her children's school and involved in various after school programs. She also volunteers in her local museum and libraries to raise awareness for reading and STEM education among children. She is a freelance writer and a book reviewer with 'Readers Favorite', 'Multicultural Children's Book Day' & 'Bookstagram Choice Awards'. So far her articles are published in Parent & Kids -North Mississippi, Think Fun and Testing Mom to name a few. Her motto is more connection & less conflict with her children, and she believes in spreading her knowledge and experiences through her parenting articles.

Facebook: https://www.facebook.com/Lovemygam/

Instagram: https://instagram.com/nupurbiswal

Chapter 34

Commonality Between Celebrations
Purvi Mangtani

"The more you praise and celebrate your life,
the more there is in life to celebrate."
- Oprah Winfrey

As a child, I used to question what makes anyone or any day worthy of remembrance? What is the purpose of rituals, and how do we benefit individually? Why isn't every day a celebration, for figuratively there are numerous battles fought every moment, and new milestones achieved in respective lives?

If the emotion of any celebration echoes equally like others in one or more ways, then can we assume that drawing comparisons and highlighting similarities between them can be an effective way of educating our children about unity?

Do you wonder if your children need to know the answers early on, so they can become more inclusive in their lives? If yes, then I hope this article can assist you in some way, for there are anecdotes shared that expanded my horizon of perceiving celebrations.

Online quests cannot always be the answer in situations that demand an emotional touch. Today, we have information a click away. There is no dearth of articles floating around in cyberspace, displaying the exhaustive list of significant days celebrated all across the globe in unique ways. But what isn't conveniently handed over to us is the ability to question the information that can help us grasp things better. No two events can entirely be the same, but there must be an emotional aspect to comprehending them for wider acceptability.

Personal experiences can be the missing pieces of the puzzle.

I am a mother of two girls. I share in-depth info on festivals with them, but I know it can never affirmatively help them understand why these are important. Moreover, I believe that our own experiences can help them understand the concept.

We are two sisters and one brother. Every year, we look forward to uniting to celebrate *Raksha Bandhan* (the knot of protection). It is a festival dedicated to sibling love, not limited to biological relationships only. Women tie *Rakhis* (decorative threads) to the wrist of their brothers, and in return, the brothers give them presents, along with a promise of protection against all odds.

My elder daughter once asked, *"We are two sisters and do not have a brother, so who will protect us, and who do we tie the Rakhi to?"* I explained that no matter what the rituals outline in a festival, the crux is going to be to honor the bond of siblings, and to stand for each other. Further, I clarified that they do not need anyone else to protect them. I encourage them to celebrate this festival by tying the thread to each other, as that symbolizes the bond between them.

In India, women celebrate festivals like *Raksha Bandhan* and *Bhai Dooj* with great affection for their brothers. In the USA, there are events like Siblings Day and Sisters Day. The rituals may vary, but the emotion will always be alike. It is the promise of protection and the affection for siblings that are the highpoints.

If you are loved in life, then there will be love in the afterlife as well.

Once my 4-year-old daughter returned from school and asked for a photo of her grandmother. My mother-in-law left for heavenly abode a couple of years ago, but she is remembered each day for her loving and compassionate disposition. During *'Shraadh'* (a ritual in India that spans over 15 days and is dedicated to honoring the loved ones that have passed away), we have her photo adorned with flowers, pay homage by offering prayers, donate food and other stuff to the needy people. We remember the life lived with pride, and contributions made in every aspect.

Since it was not that time of the year *(Shraadh)*, I asked my daughter why she wanted a photo of her grandmother. To which she replied with her glossy eyes and a priceless smile that knew no respite, *"Mom there is an altar decorated in my school. All students can place the picture of their loved ones, who are in heaven now. I want my grandmother to visit me and meet my friends."*

I was gob smacked but also overwhelmed to see that regardless of diversity, emotions find their way to ring a bell at the doorsteps of your heart. It was the *'Day of the Dead'* festival of Mexico that was being celebrated in her school. During this event (*Día de Muertos*), altars are decorated to welcome the spirits of loved ones back to earth. Candles, bright orange marigolds, and decorations like intricately cut tissue paper banners, guide the spirits back to earth, where they find their favorite foods, liquors, and things that were important to them. Amidst all the variances, she thought of her grandmother, and that deeply touched our hearts. As it is said, *"We live only once is wrong. We die only once, but we live every day."* People who are loved in life will continue to live eternally in the hearts and minds of others.

So the similarities between the two rituals are honoring the loved ones that have departed, in the company of friends and families, showcasing the value of the deceased members, adornment, and chants of wishes and prayers. These comparisons have helped me teach my children to be kind, approachable, and get admired for their deeds in life. It is a precious platform to perform correctly and be remembered fondly, even after our mission in life is accomplished.

When it concerns love, do not look for the box to think inside or outside of it.

We had the opportunity of living in parts of north India before moving to the Middle East. That is where I first experienced the festival of *Karwa Chauth*. Not surprised by why my mother chose to follow the same, I witnessed this celebration at my house every year. On this day, married women pray for the longevity and prosperity of their partners. They observe fasts from sunrise to moonrise, wear red to express affection, and say brief prayers. Later, they break their fasts in the evening by looking at the moon or its reflection in the water first, and then their husbands'. Women usually celebrate this in groups to arrange the rituals perfectly, so it becomes a joyous gathering followed by appetizing meals.

I grew up with this ceremony ingrained in my heart. It described the essence of love for your partner and was the epitome of romance. After marriage, I moved to Mumbai (India) and marched into a family that had a unique set of rituals, compared to the ones I had observed earlier. They had traditions quite different from what I had witnessed within my bubble. Women here majorly celebrated *Teej*, which is precisely the same as *Karwa Chauth*. It is observed for the wellbeing and long life of their spouse. I wondered if I must switch from what seemed somewhat similar, but celebrated on another day with different customs.

My marital family has always been extremely accommodating, and a believer of values more than the events or rituals. I had the freedom to pursue what resonated with my own emotions and ideology. The idea here is to see that the traditions will change as

212

you traverse places. What will not change are the values, the themes, and the passion to follow the customs, no matter how trying they may seem.

If *Karwa Chauth* and *Teej* from the *Hindu* culture underline on expressing love for your partner, then would it be wrong to see Valentine's day place itself in the same genre? It is also the occasion when people show their affection for another person. Although not fasting or praying, the soul of this day is also Love!

My daughters can comprehend the essence of care and affection well. Showcasing these festivals helps instill the value of love in life and the significance of expression.

Learning is an eternal journey - travel the extra mile, and you will always find something niche to learn.

As I had mentioned in my previous chapter, about the cultural tremor I endured due to moving from India to the Middle East, and that included the celebratory wave too. For instance, at some places in the middle east, it was considered intolerable to eat or drink in public during the holy month of *Ramadan* when people observed fasting. There were times when it was difficult for me because firstly, it wasn't a part of my culture, and secondly, restraint is mastered over a period of time. It takes a lot of endurance to gain victory over your sense of hunger!

Once during Ramadan, while I was with my work team consisting mostly of Muslims, I vividly remember someone mentioning a person warned and fined for eating in front of other fasting colleagues. It did concern me for a reasonable time until one day when a small but compassionate moment changed my viewpoint.

While I was at work, I developed a throbbing headache due to rising fever, and I didn't have an escape route due to the increased workload. I believe my predicament must have been apparent, but also the conundrum of my mind was making it worse. My bubble of all negatives popped when my reporting manager offered me dates to eat with a cup of coffee. He was a local observing the fast religiously, so I looked at him confused and was unable to gage his intention behind doing so. Before the war of words in my head could go on any further, he said, *"You look extremely pale and unwell. Why should you have to exercise fasting when it is not a part of your faith? Please do not exert yourself and take some medicine after you consume this."*

I could feel a lump in my throat, but my mind was reluctant to take the step, fearing to regret later. He further said, *"My faith and values teach me to endure hunger and sacrifice my privileges, to honor the Almighty. That does not mean I must have the convenience of 'no food or water' around me during that time. Then where is my ability to control in this whole arrangement? So please go ahead and feel well."*

As humans, we are social beings who value relations and affection. If someone before you is offering their privileges and pleasures to honor their faith, then it is equally commendable to forfeit your comforts and endure hunger, to appreciate their sacrifices.

Coming back to the commonality between celebrations, you will be surprised to know that in India, the Hindu culture has a festival known as *Navratri*, which spans over nine nights, and the devotees observe fasts for all days. It is observed for different reasons in various parts of India. It also includes sacrificing pleasures like food and other luxuries. Similarly, Christians observe Lent (Season of 40 days) before Easter. Lent doesn't require Christians to fast; although, it does ask them to give up something, which can be seen in the light of self-discipline.

The common theme here is endurance, the victory of Good over Evil, recital of the legend, chanting, charity, self-reflection, and celebrations in the end. So in some way, it can be assumed that the spirit is similar for these rituals specified above

Distance from being a Kid to being a Kind adult isn't straightforward, but the journey is imperative for happier living and worth every effort.

As parents, we often partner with the festivals and cultures in our endeavors of teaching our children the principles of a good life. For instance, courtesy the eagerness to be in Santa's good books, get the desired gifts from the personal wish list, be tagged as everyone's favorite - our daughter has beautifully embraced the essence of Christmas. She is shaping up to be appreciative and kind to others around her.

Doesn't the attribute of being kind and grateful also resonate with the message of Thanksgiving? Thanksgiving is also a 'Harvest Festival' that is celebrated all across the world. It is observed at varying times of the year, depending on the main harvest of a given region. For instance, the most popular harvest festivals from India are *Makar Sankranti*, *Akshay Tritiya*, and *Gudi Padwa*. The list of names that echo with Thanksgiving or harvest festivals from all across the world is endless. The ways of celebrating may be unique, but the purpose is somewhat similar. To be grateful for what we have and to pray for future prosperity.

By drawing parallels from various rituals, I have been able to infuse awareness of the diverse cultures for my daughters. Concurrently, I have also been able to explain to them why it is important to be grateful for not just one day, but consistently!

Peace is when there is unity in the understanding of diversity and the commonality in ethics.

We celebrate, to remember our heritage and showcase them in a festive way to our generations, so that the cultural beliefs, important guidelines, and teachings are not lost. We make way for festivities because it allows us to give respect and show passion for what matters. Family, friends, food, traditions, music, prayers, and above all, willingness to stand in harmony to enjoy the moments. I believe the similarities are quite evident, if there is a desire to perceive them in the mutual interest of mankind.

I wish for my daughters to understand and appreciate the connections between celebrations, but before that, I want them to understand that it is not limited to the customs and characteristics set by society. The ideologies and heritages will continue to function as our moral guidelines. I wish for them to learn that life is a celebration, and each day a moment to revere.

There isn't a better way of finding amity than by understanding the relatable attributes, and by educating our future generations about the same. This world is diverse, but we must respect all, for we are all a part of one Universe!

ABOUT PURVI MANGTANI

With an MBA degree in Sales and Marketing and a prosperous corporate span of 12 years, Purvi Mangtani (also known as Leena Asnanie) has a strong acumen for persuasive speaking and creative writing. Purvi is an Art and Travel Aficionado. She is currently exploring her affection for storytelling through photography and passion for mixed media through her new venture @cuesfromhues. Besides artworks, content curation as a freelancer, and parenting, she also enjoys writing her travel anecdotes on Instagram @milesupheart. She is a global citizen, currently based in Chicago, Illinois with her husband and two children. She believes that while it is imperative to adapt to changing times, one should never drift away from their aspirations.

Instagram: https://instagram.com/milesupheart

Instagram: https://instagram.com/cuesfromhues

Chapter 35

Cultural Appreciation
Vs
Appropriation
Aditi Wardhan Singh

The Cambridge Dictionary defines cultural appropriation as - *"The act of taking or using things from a culture that is not your own, especially without showing that you understand or respect this culture."*

My attention got drawn to this topic when I saw influencers using *Namaste* as *Namaslay* as a motto to sell their classes, on tshirts. It brought me to think about the yoga teachers who are not Indian but who say Namaste, before and after class, just for the added ambience. They do not even bother to understand the meaning.

Once you start noticing such things, they are everywhere. Yoga itself has been morphed into goat yoga, wine yoga etc. People take any one aspect of another culture that is unique and add it to their offering, celebration, or venture etc. to give the attendee or consumer that added experience. Most of the time this goes unnoticed because the appropriation being done is unintentional and often used as a crutch for added flair to make people smile.

This is such a touchy topic and very difficult to define with clear boundaries because there is a thin line between experiencing another culture and mocking it or using it for your benefit on a whim.

Like when a popular social media influencer (not of Indian or Hindu heritage) had a *Hindu* wedding and put out the video for likes and comments. It was not just that they wore the clothes, but they did all the rituals and traditions (again with no understanding) in the name of cultural appreciation. It was offensive, at least to a viewer like me who takes great pride in their heritage and the meaning behind traditions, that someone would use my culture as a prop for increasing their views online. Going to the limits of saying, *"This is just us enjoying Hindu traditions."*

Now, I am the first person to incorporate different festivals into my life. We try to learn about and make memorable moments of all celebrations, but I am most mindful of reading about what we are celebrating and what the traditions mean. I am happy to report, every year we as a family learn something new about cultures around the world, especially our *own* heritage.

So how do you know the difference?

This book has many, many ways in which you can develop a culturally sensitive mindset through conversation and mindfulness. It is so much more important to talk to children about cultural appropriation for that is when someone might take offense.

Appreciation **is to get educated about a culture so you can better understand it. This can quickly transform into appropriation, the moment you try to benefit from this. Appropriation is where you take from others and then put yourself in a position of authority.**

Appreciation **has you looking to others to guide the conversation. It keeps you clearly in the role of a learner.**

Case in point, the below examples.

Cultural appreciation -

- Wearing henna at a friend's wedding
- Participating in a friend's traditional function
- Reading about and incorporating some parts of culture into your home celebrations
- Trying a folk dance or dancing to a trending song. Learning a new aspect i.e cooking, dancing, music.

Cultural appropriation -

- When people use/substitute cultural traditions during pop videos, weddings, or events for photo ops.
- When you take *Hindu* gods, symbols and add them to fabrics in the name of fashion.
- When you see people defining themselves as *"gurus"* or "monks".

As with all interactions, the fine line is defined by respect and how much you are taking.

So, how do we teach our children about the same?

By having these conversations early and talking to them about the many aspects you experience as a family. Build a bridge between mindfulness and how you respect a culture while experiencing parts of it. Help kids identify the difference early and stop them from overstepping their welcome into another culture's identity. Or worse, having the next generations morph a language, tradition or cultural aspects such that the whole identity gets lost.

Below are the aspects that one needs to be thoughtful about -

Food

Eating a cuisine does not make you an expert on a culture. So often you hear people saying, "I just love Indian food. Butter chicken and Kadhai paneer are my favorite." As if, eating Mughlai food at an Indian restaurant is a stamp of cultural appreciation. Indian food is so much more what is most ordered at restaurants.

Cuisine often exemplifies cultural exchange at its best. However, in instances where someone of the dominant culture is profiting off the customs and culture of a nondominant culture, without the occurrence of any sort of cultural (or monetary) exchange, it gets into dicey territory. For e.g., Indo-Chinese was earlier known as Chinese food in India. It is well loved by most Indians around the world but most people, especially people from China have no idea that there is such a popular take on their cuisine. I remember when as a child, our relative took us to an authentic Chinese restaurant, my entire family was shocked to see what real Chinese food was like. It is only recently that people started referring to it as Indo-Chinese, thus giving back Chinese food it's identity.

Music

One can see the overlap in a lot of popular music. The cultural overlap is so vehement that true authenticity has been lost. Many artists do not even bother creating original content anymore. The problem often lies in the fact that, whether it is the artist's intention or not, certain looks and sounds and "aesthetics" are automatically deemed more palatable by society, when displayed on or by someone who is white.

Accessories

Wearing headdresses, blackface, kimonos, and other clothing symbols, and facets of other cultures. Trends like cornrows and wearing chopsticks as hair accessories "borrow" from black and Asian cultures. The latter being inappropriate and inaccurate.

Using sacred symbols for non-spiritual reasons is a big one in this case.

Themed Events

During Halloween, you see many people going as historical characters from various backgrounds. It is not enough that they wear the costume, but they paint their faces to match. Or you see someone wearing an Indian dress as a Halloween outfit. Someone's cultural heritage is NOT a costume. Additionally, parties in which the theme is something stereotypically associated with a specific group of people, goes beyond cultural appropriation in just being blatantly racist. Having parties that are in a theme, just for an opportunity to take fun photos so you can show online is inappropriate. It's virtually impossible to go dressed as an entire ethnicity or culture, without playing heavily into some harmful stereotypes.

Here are ways to help your kids think about the difference between appreciating a culture and appropriating it.

- Do not just incorporate a tradition into your life without educating yourself about it.

- Be intentional. Before you do anything, think about what you are doing and who it may impact.

- Ask yourself, are you being respectful or just imitating for fun?

- Think about the stereotype you may be helping carry forward.

- Do not do things just for a photo opportunity to post online.

- Make the effort to understand your own culture and its relationship to other cultures throughout history.

- Be a student always. Do not assume you know everything, just because you experience part of a culture.

221

- Do not fear asking questions before imbibing or partaking in a tradition.

One needs to remember that explaining this fine line to someone with a closed mind is impossible. Your job, as a participant is to learn, and not educate about something you have just learned about.

The beginning of being respectful of all cultures and anti-racism education begins with an open mind, and the willingness to accept mistakes we may have made in the past. Being a lifelong learner of world cultures and growing your multicultural family with a global mindset.

ABOUT ADITI WARDHAN SINGH

Multi award winning author and self-publishing coach, Aditi is an authoritative voice on cultural sensitivity and self-empowerment. She founded RaisingWorldChildren.com, an online and print publication for multicultural families and authored the parenting book Strong Roots Have No Fear. From a childhood of feeling like the Girl from Nowhere, she grew to believing that we belong everywhere. Her books How Our Skin Sparkles, Sparkles of Joy, Small or Tall - We Sparkle After All teach kids about acceptance - of self and others.

In her spare time, a trained Indian classical dancer in Kathak & Bharatnatyam, Aditi likes to choreograph dance recitals to be performed at local festivals & have impromptu dance parties with her children.

Website: https://raisingworldchildren.com/

Instagram: https://www.instagram.com/raisingworldchildren/

NOTABLE THOUGHT LEADERS FROM AROUND THE WORLD

Please find below more thought leaders around the world, much like the curator of this book **Aditi Wardhan Singh and the featured contributors,** who are diligently creating resources that multicultural families can benefit from towards building diversity, inclusion and conversations against divisions of all kinds.

Varya Sanina-Garmroud is raising multicultural children in China, blogging about life as an expat parent and educator.

Creativeworldofvarya.com

Frances Evans started blogging about her multicultural family living and discovering the world through her son's eyes.

discoveringtheworldthroughmysonseyes.com/

Adee Sasa shares spanish books for kids around the world. Build multilingualism through books with this cool website.

kidsspanishbookclub.blogspot.com/

Maria Wen Adcock runs a parenting blog that celebrates bicultural and multicultural families with a focus on Asian culture.

BiculturalMama.com

FB Smit has the Eeyagi Tales blog. It has Korean and Asian content from How Chopsticks differ from China, Korea and Japan, as well as children's book reviews

eeyagitales.com/

Elisavet Arkolaki is passionate about travel and inspired by global learning. She raises her own children in between countries, cultures, and languages. She's the author of 'Where am I from?', 'Happiness Street' (available in several bilingual editions), and the curator of 'How to Raise Confident Multicultural Children'.

maltamum.com

Adrienne Hayes Demirelli shares advice, language activities and books that have contributed to our three kids' success in six languages in order to inspire and encourage your own family's multilingual and multicultural journey.

Https://themultilingualhome.com

MaryAnne Kochenderfer was raised in five countries on three continents, and she is passionate about global education. Her blog features a world cultures series focused on introducing children to the beauty of global diversity, as well as other educational activities, crafts, and family travel tips.

mamasmiles.com

Greatfamilyreads.com

Vanessa Ruis is the creator of Embracing Diversity. It is committed to providing families with the tools they need to begin embracing cultural, racial, and linguistic diversity today, in order to help pave the way for a better tomorrow.

https://familiesembracingdiversity.com/

Amanda Hsiung Blodgett is the creator of Miss Panda Chinese. It is a bilingual education website featuring resources for parents and educators to guide early language learners to acquire the Chinese language, explore Chinese culture, and connect with the world!

misspandachinese.com/

Kay Tarapolsi runs a handcrafts and vibrant Arab world via craft tutorials, downloads, book lists and other resources that teach about the Middle East and North Africa.

A Crafty Arab

Charu Chhitwal is making an effort to connect saucy and unapologetically self-loving moms. They have recently started a successful fb-live show Ketchupmoms Let's Talk, where we discuss everything from stressed moms to contraceptives! Founder Charu Chhitwal is mommy to twins who is a big-time foodie.

ketchupmoms.com

Vicki Michela Garlock offers religious literacy and interfaith education resources for families, schools, and churches. Her publications include: We All Have Sacred Spaces -- a kids' book exploring sacred spaces from 7 different faith traditions -- and Interfaith Made Easy: Peace -- a 4-volume (for 4 age groups), 15-

lesson plan curriculum with stories, crafts, and activities from 9 different faith traditions.

faithseekerkids.com

Acknowledgements

A special thank you to Minali Bajaj Syed, managing editor of RWC, for being co-editor on this project, while valiantly homeschooling. Every woman in this book is a powerhouse and united, at a most difficult time. When the world was battling racism, the Coronavirus, and various social issues, these women came together to stand tall together, through their words.

My heart is always overwhelmed by the support I get for the work I do but none of it would be possible without the inspiration and support of my kids and husband. A special mention today must go to our respective families back in India, that have ensured that we are diverse and inclusive in our mindset.

Aditi's Books

Strong Roots Have No Fear

Sparkling Me Series (Children's Books)

How Our Skin Sparkles

Sparkles of Joy

Small or Tall, We Sparkle After All

My Time to Sparkle (July 2021)

Raising the Social Mindset (Coming 2022)

Founded in 2017, RaisingWorldChildren.com is a multicultural family resource for building cultural sensitivity and self-empowerment in multicultural families everywhere.

Email contact@raisignworldchildren.com to connect with Aditi W. Singh for your writing, self-publishing, or book marketing needs.

Made in the USA
Coppell, TX
22 June 2021

57889420R00136